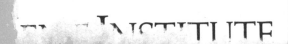

IMAGES OF WARTIME

BRITISH ART AND ARTISTS OF WORLD WAR I

IMAGES OF WARTIME
BRITISH ART AND ARTISTS OF WORLD WAR I

NIGEL VINEY

Pictures from the Collection of the
Imperial War Museum

DAVID & CHARLES

Acknowledgements are due to the staff of the Imperial War Museum; in particular, to the most helpful librarians who staff the Reading Room; to Angela Weight, Keeper of Art; to members of the Department of Art, notably Pauline Allwright, Michael Moody and Jenny Wood; and to Christopher Dowling.

Frontispiece: William McMillan, *A Canadian Infantryman*
Contents page: Henry Alfred Pegram, *Field Marshal Lord Allenby*

British Library Cataloguing in Publication Data
Viney, Nigel
Images of wartime: British art and artists of World War I.
1. Great Britain. Paintings. Special subjects: War
I. Title
758.99

ISBN 0-7153-9790-7

Text copyright © Nigel Viney 1991
Illustrations copyright © The Imperial War Museum 1991

The right of Nigel Viney to be identified as
author of this work has been asserted by him in accordance
with the Copyright, Designs and Patents Act 1988.

Book designed by Michael Head

Typeset by Ace Filmsetting Ltd, Frome, Somerset
and printed in Singapore by CS Graphics Pte Ltd
for David & Charles plc
Brunel House   Newton Abbot   Devon

CONTENTS

LIST OF PLATES

FOREWORD

A year or two back, researching for the *Shell Guide to the Great Paintings of England*, I visited every permanent collection of pictures in the country. In the course of this highly enjoyable work, I was not able to see any of the art collection of the Imperial War Museum: the place was deep in the reconstruction work which has brought into being the present magnificent galleries, and as a consequence none of the huge collection of paintings could be displayed.

This was a grievous misfortune. My description of the collection was correspondingly inadequate. But I became more and more intrigued by what I had been unable to see; the more I read about the collection, the more reproductions I saw, the more my interest grew. In the end, it seemed, the only way to resolve this paradoxical situation was to write another book, devoted entirely to works in the Museum.

It very soon became apparent that this would have to be restricted to World War I, if the book was to have any chance at all of doing justice to the paintings, drawings and sculpture in the Collection. But this book is not by any means a catalogue. It is a personal selection, designed, within the limits of a modest-sized volume, to give the reader an idea of the scope of the Collection, to indicate some of the highlights, to explain briefly how it came into being, and to say something about the backgrounds and careers of some of the artists involved, and how their wartime experiences affected them.

Although I have had a great deal of willing help from members of the staff of the Museum in putting this book together, the views I express are mine, not those of the Museum. The book is an invitation to readers to come and see the Collection; it is an aperitif, an appetite-whetter, and it is also a signpost, pointing in the direction of what to look out for.

The Collection is magnificent. Pictures from World War I are not to be found elsewhere in Britain, so it is certainly unique in this respect. It can also be thought of as uniquely compelling and powerful, a window onto the everyday conditions, the unimaginable horrors endured and the courage shown during that appalling conflict.

PRE-WAR BRITAIN

After the relative tranquillity of the Victorian era, Britain in the early years of the twentieth century was subject to a number of outbreaks of violent and passionate feeling. For us today, looking back on them as part of our recent history, it is tempting to view these events as harbingers of the terrible violence of the Great War of 1914–18 – to perceive the violence which emerged in the reign of Edward VII and in the period from 1910 to 1914 as presaging and foreshadowing the catastrophic war in which unimaginable destruction would take place on a far greater scale than all previous wars.

Winston Churchill, by 1914 already an experienced politican, identified the Jameson Raid of 1896 as the first violent event in a successive chain of violence. The raid, absurdly ill-judged and ineptly handled, heralded the Boer War of 1899. This war, in its turn, led to the 'Khaki' election of 1901, one of the occasions in British history when patriotic feelings, enhanced by the atmosphere of war, have served to confirm the ruling party – in this case the Tories – in power.

The Protectionist Movement and the uproar about Chinese labour in South Africa followed, events which helped to re-unite the Liberal Party (then fractured for a number of reasons) and culminated in a Liberal majority in the general election of 1906.

As there was, at the time, a massive Tory majority in the House of Lords, Parliamentary trouble of some kind could scarcely have been avoided. The catalyst was Lloyd George's Budget of 1909; this was accompanied by language of an unprecedented violence delivered in skilfully demagogic tones which were themselves never previously associated with a minister of the Crown. The uproar over this Budget led directly to the Parliament Bill, the two general elections of 1910, and the cabinet threat to create several hundred Liberal peers if required. After these elections the Liberals in the House of Commons depended on the votes of the Irish Nationalists. Irish Home Rule, an issue which had been dormant since the death of Gladstone in 1898, once again became dominant in British politics. The struggle on this issue took the country near to the brink of civil war in the spring and summer of 1914 – a crisis strikingly exemplified by the 'Curragh Mutiny' of that eventful year.

Sir Jacob Epstein, *The Tin Hat*
Bronze, 13½ ins
The jaunty angle of the steel helmet perhaps helped to draw public attention to this work when it was first exhibited.

Violence in these years not only emerged in political activity, but also took other forms. Industrial unrest and strikes made themselves widely felt on a scale unknown in British history. The South Wales miners' strike of 1910 affected 30,000 men; in the following year there was an epidemic of strikes affecting shipyard workers and dockers throughout that famously hot summer; and there was a general railway strike in 1912.

Violence could be seen all too plainly, too, in the activities of the Suffragettes. From the perspective of the 1990s it seems utterly absurd that there should have been no votes at all for women in national elections, when there was universal male suffrage; moreover, women who were ratepayers could not only vote in local elections but could sit on local councils. At the time, however, eminent men produced one idiotic argument after another in defence of the status quo; their numbers included all the members of the Liberal Cabinet, widely regarded as a brilliant assembly. As more and more women became increasingly frustrated and impatient, it was only to be expected that militancy would emerge. Initial action, largely on the level of schoolgirl pranks, were treated with shocked horror and the heaviest of hands. Greater damage followed, cruel repressions followed in their turn, and real tragedies were the result. Nothing like this had ever happened before. It was not until 1918, when women over the age of thirty received a vote, that the barriers began to fall.

It is true that progress was made in social matters in the early years of the century. But although estate duty had begun as far back as 1894, and was extended in 1907, by 1914 something like two-thirds of the wealth of the country was concentrated in the hands of less than a hundredth of the population. Half a dozen new universities were inaugurated in Edwardian days, but the total number of university students was still very low as compared with, for example, Germany. Parliamentary salaries, very modest in size, were started in 1911, largely because of the emergence of the Labour party. It had hardly been noticed in the Liberal landslide of 1906 that twenty-nine Labour members had been elected, making Labour a force to be reckoned with for the first time.

Feelings ran very high in those days. Campaigns were carried on at fever pitch in an atmosphere of continuous excitement, in newspapers which were themselves, for the first time, sensationalist in tone. Matters such as Tariff Reform, a name invented to make Protectionism sound more respectable, were passionately debated. Families were split and old friends ceased to speak to each other over the possibility that the House of Lords would defend the Parliament Bill, and people stood in their thousands in Parliament Square until late in the night to learn how the vital vote had gone. The possibility of Home Rule for Ireland, always a fruitful source of dispute, raised passions to the point where

private armies were illegally raised and trained, with former Cabinet ministers openly preaching civil war.

Germany was under the personal leadership of Kaiser Wilhelm II, Queen Victoria's eldest grandson, whose feelings about Britain combined awed admiration with pathological jealousy. Germany had a small fleet, very few overseas possessions, and an enormous army which was the largest in Europe and rightly believed to be well organised and efficient. In 1900 Germany publicly declared its intention of building up a fighting fleet large enough to challenge the Royal Navy. This naturally caused alarm, and Britain made strenuous efforts to maintain the supremacy of its navy at all costs, building ships to match the German programme and modernising the fleet to maintain quality as well as quantity. This naval race was carried on in a highly charged atmosphere, the Kaiser's often hysterical outbursts being matched by equally violent language in the jingoistic British press. Violence was in the air in Britain in the years before 1914.

THE ARTS BEFORE 1914

The ferment in public affairs in Britain, so intense and so pervasive, was reflected to some extent in the arts during the Edwardian period and in the brief span of King George's reign until the outbreak of war. As in the 1890s, often thought of purely as a period of decadence and of art for art's sake, there was in fact a wide variety of activity in all the arts in these years. Certainly the voice of the twentieth century was to be heard early on, even if it was not always heard by many.

In literature, H. G. Wells had made his name in the 1890s with his powerful and popular scientific fantasies; now he had turned to rich comedies and to novels with social themes, such as *Ann Veronica*. The work of D. H. Lawrence had started to appear in 1911, and *Sons and Lovers* was published in 1913. James Joyce, too, had begun to make his unique voice heard, *Dubliners* being published in 1914. Hugh Walpole and Somerset Maugham were both active and successful. George Moore, Joseph Conrad and Henry James were at work. The quiet but penetrating voice of E. M. Forster was already audible, and Arnold Bennett was busy throughout the period, as usual combining great industry with great integrity. More widely read was the older John Galsworthy, whose *The Man of Property* was published in 1906; other popular writers included A. E. W. Mason, Robert Hichens, Edgar Wallace, and Baroness Orczy.

Some fiction writers were equally at home in the theatre: Bennett, Galsworthy and Maugham all wrote plays, finding an immediate response to their work and, in some cases, a lasting reputation. Pinero had ceased to write but J. M. Barrie was very active as was George Bernard Shaw. His plays had started to appear in the 1890s, usually in private performances, sometimes abroad; by 1914 he had become highly successful as a playwright and his plays endure to the present, speaking as they do with a contemporary twentieth-century accent.

It would be all too easy for anyone today to think of the music of the Edwardian age as essentially exemplified by the Brahms-like harmonies of Edward Elgar, far and away the most considerable figure in British music since Handel. But, again, this would be a superficial, easy judgement, over-simplifying a more complex situation. Sir Thomas Beecham's Covent Garden opera season of 1910 included both Richard Strauss's *Elektra* and his *Feuersnot*. The harsh cadences of Stravinsky were to be heard in London in 1911, when his music for *The Firebird* emerged in the Russian Ballet season with which Diaghilev electrified a public which had seen nothing like it before. The effect of this particular often-described performance lay not just in the skill and panache of the superbly trained dancers, nor in the brand-new music of Stravinsky, but also in the bright, bold, flat colours of the stage décor, especially that designed by Alexandre Benois and Léon Bakst.

In all the circumstances of the time, it is scarcely surprising that the décor of the Russian Ballet should have been so immediately effective. For the general public, or rather the theatre-going, ballet-going public, the visual arts meant the Royal Academy's Summer Exhibition, a show which was in those days inextricably entangled with the social 'London season'; indeed the Academy's private view marked the opening of this season. It is not too much to say that the Royal Academy was in those days singing the same songs, so to speak, as it had sung for fifty years past, and was in fact to continue singing for at least another thirty years. Greatly accomplished as many late Victorian and Edwardian artists were (a fact which is only recently being reflected in sale-room prices), they were emphatically not innovators. To find real innovators among the ranks of the Academicians one would have to look back a very long way to the days of Turner, who died in 1851, and Constable, who died in Queen Victoria's accession year of 1837.

This is not to say that there were not both artists and collectors who were very well aware of the Impressionists (whose activities dated from the 1870s), and of those who came to be labelled the Post-Impressionists. But to see and study Impressionist pictures, and to buy examples, it was necessary to go to Paris; and, in Paris, the pictures had to be sought out in dealers' shops and in studios rather than at the Salon. It is an astonishing fact that Roger Fry, the foremost art critic of the time and director of New York's Metropolitan Museum from 1905 to 1910, did not even see a painting by Cézanne until 1906, the year of Cézanne's death and certainly thirty years after his pictures were first exhibited. It has to be recalled, also, that popular books on artistic subjects did not exist, and that colour reproduction was in its infancy. It was all too easy for cultural isolation to flourish.

Fry's famous 1910 London exhibition entitled 'Manet and the Post-Impressionists' was, hardly surprisingly, as sensational as the Russian Ballet was to be a year later. It caused something very like hysteria, as the London public was seeing work by such artists as Seurat, Signac, Cézanne, Gauguin and van Gogh for the first time. Two years later a further exhibition was organised, with Braque and Picasso included, and had similarly sensational results.

All these names were familiar enough to those British artists who had studied and worked in France. A number of these were linked with W. R. Sickert who, along with his exact contemporary Wilson Steer – they were both born in 1860, and both died in 1942 – is thought of as the leading British Impressionist. Sickert, who was not to be elected a Royal Academician (RA) until 1934, had adapted Impressionist techniques to his own vision, so that his pictures are always very much his own – usually low and quiet in tone. Unlike the first Impressionists, he disliked the countryside, preferring townscapes and delighting in music-hall scenes. The artists linked with Sickert in the Camden Town Group, formed in 1911, included Harold Gilman, Spencer Gore, Augustus John, Henry Lamb and Lucien Pissarro (who was the son of the great Impressionist Camille Pissarro, and had settled in England). This group was to set the tone of British art for the next forty years.

Other influential forces included the New English Art Club, little known until its exhibition of 1906. Robert Ross's Carfax Gallery, which he purchased in 1901, had influence out of all proportion to its tiny size. Hugh Lane, a 'gentleman-dealer' whose private collection included pictures by Manet and Renoir, is said to have 'dragged taste forward by twenty or thirty years'. The National Arts-Collection Fund was founded in 1903, the Contemporary Art Society in 1910; *Burlington* magazine, founded in 1903, was bold enough the following year to refer to van Gogh as 'a great master'.

In sharp contrast to Britain, continental Europe was, artistically, in boiling ferment in the pre-war years, with Paris the focal point of new ideas and revolutionary movements. Cubism, foreshadowed by Cézanne and heralded by Picasso's *Demoiselles d'Avignon* of 1906–7, had arrived, flourished and largely faded away by 1914. Fauvism had been through a similar process of flowering and withering a few years earlier. Neither of these two movements had elicited much response in Britain. Futurism was another movement which bubbled to the surface at this time; perhaps because, unusually, it had not started in Paris, it found little favour in France. Formally announced by Filippo Tommaso Marinetti in 1909, it succeeded in crossing the Channel – there was a Futurist exhibition in London in 1912.

These developments were not without effect in avant-garde circles in Britain. A period of study in Paris was, at this time, a normal (though not inevitable) part of a young artist's education, and many were influenced by the excitements and innovations to be seen in that city. This was most strikingly exemplified by the Vorticist movement, which had the distinction of being unique to Britain, and which owed its existence to the singular artist and writer Wyndham Lewis. Both Cubism and Futurism had some influence on Vorticism. As well as attacking the sentimentality which underlay much Royal Academy art, Vorticism celebrated violence, energy and the machine, its revolutionary fervour being expressed in abstract compositions of bold lines and sharp angles.

Along with Wyndham Lewis the artists David Bomberg, C. R. W. Nevinson, Edward Wadsworth, William Roberts – then very young – and Jacob Epstein were all involved to some extent, even if only briefly and tentatively. If Vorticism's violence heralded and pre-reflected, in a dramatic way, the appalling violence of war which was so swiftly to follow, the war itself effectively killed Vorticism. Real life seemed, for once, to imitate art, on a mockingly gigantic scale.

THE OUTBREAK OF WAR

When war came, it came with appalling suddenness, almost out of the blue, at the August Bank Holiday weekend.*

In those days the Balkans were a hotbed of small and quarrelsome states, some of them linked by alliances to the three large neighbours who bordered their territories – the Austro-Hungarian empire, the Russian empire and the Turkish, or Ottoman, empire. Austria-Hungary was Germany's ally; Russia had understandings with both France and Britain; Turkey was viewed with suspicion by both Austria-Hungary and Russia. There had been violent local upheavals in the Balkans in 1908 and again in 1912, linked to the break-up, actual or impending, of the Austro-Hungarian and Ottoman empires.

Franz-Josef, the Austrian Emperor, was eighty-three. His heir (the Archduke Franz-Ferdinand) was assassinated on 28 June 1914 by an anarchist who sympathised with Serbia and whose plans had been laid in Serbia. Austria, which had been awaiting such an opportunity and was egged on by Germany, seized the chance to attack Serbia. This happened on 28 July. Up till this moment, all had seemed as though it was just another Balkan squabble. But Serbia was allied to Russia, and Russia now started to mobilise. This in turn resulted in German mobilisation, and that led inexorably to mobilisation in France.

The British Cabinet had been embroiled in the harsh, bitter and very dangerous problems of Ireland. According to Churchill, then First Lord of the Admiralty, when the Cabinet met on 24 July it 'toiled around the muddy byways of Fermanagh and Tyrone'. It was at the end of this meeting that Grey, the Foreign Secretary, read out the Austrian note to Serbia. This was couched in such terms that it seemed certain that the note would be rejected, thus making war, if not inevitable, then highly probable. But should Britain become involved? Neither the ties with Russia nor those with France specifically required Britain to declare war, though this was implied. Many of the Cabinet were anti-

* An uncle of mine treasured for the rest of his days a wish-you-were-here holiday postcard sent by his mother from Switzerland on 1 August 1914, which had as a postscript: 'Father thinks nothing of this war scare'. His parents were unable to return to England for several months.

Sir William Orpen, *The Big Crater, No 2*
Oil, 30 × 36 ins
The position of this crater – a relic of earlier fighting, subsequently marked by a temporary grave – is now obscure.

militaristic, some were pro-German in sympathy, some had been pro-Boer fifteen years earlier, and one was a convinced pacifist.

The Cabinet agonised for a week, hoping against hope. The turning point was the German invasion of Belgium and Luxembourg, whose neutrality was guaranteed by the larger European powers. For many years Britain had sought to avoid entanglements on the Continent, but equally it viewed with dismay the presence of a dominant power in the Low Countries.

The tension, violence, even hysteria which was manifest in British domestic affairs and perhaps reflected in some aspects of British art, is also to be discerned in international affairs in the immediate pre-war period. The successive steps which led to the outbreak of the catastrophic and devastating war certainly have an air of hysteria about them. Equally they have a nightmarish quality in which the statesmen involved seem to have been sleep-walking, plodding through a diplomatic ritual which had often been gone through before, with nobody having any real understanding of the actual and terrible possibilities.

Hardly anywhere was the true nature of the war foreseen. 'You will be home before the leaves have fallen from the trees,' Kaiser Wilhelm II told his departing soldiers, voicing in characteristically picturesque

Paul Nash, *Wire*
Ink, pastel and watercolour, 18¾ × 24½ ins
Paul Nash had the gift of making inanimate objects, even such unpromising
material as barbed wire, into images of strange and haunting beauty.

language a widespread feeling, held by responsible people all over Europe, that the conflict would be short, if bloody. The wars fought by the Germans in the previous century – even the Franco-Prussian War of 1870–1 – had been so, and the word *blitzkrieg* had been coined to describe them.

Few foresaw the slaughter which would be caused by automatic weapons, by modern explosives, and by barbed-wire entanglements, still less the effect of poison gases or of aerial bombardments; nor the way in which the railway systems of Europe could first move the vast Continental conscript armies and then keep them supplied. Nor did anybody foresee the real privations which would affect the whole British nation, nor the immense effort of national will which would be needed to sustain the war effort for months and years ahead.

Marshal Foch, eventually the Supreme Commander of the Allies (as the French and British were known) on the Western Front, had said emphatically in 1910 that 'The aircraft is all very well for sport; for the army it is useless'. His colleague, the French Inspector-General of Infantry, said, in the same year, that 'The machine-gun will not make the slightest difference to anything'. The French infantry went to war in 1914 in the red képis and red trousers of the Second Empire, which were actually designed to make the troops *more* visible, with the object of striking terror into the hearts of the enemy. Officers wore pipe-clayed white gloves; cuirassiers rode with polished breastplates, exactly like those still worn by the Household Cavalry in Britain on ceremonial occasions.

In all Europe, no nation was more ignorant than Britain, whose forces had not been engaged on the Continent since the Battle of Waterloo ninety-nine years earlier. Britain had an enormous navy but its army was a small professional force, much of it stationed in peacekeeping roles throughout the empire, especially in India. In fact only five or six divisions could initially be mustered to send across the Channel to France.

Astonishing as it now seems, Britain had no Secretary of State for War at the outbreak of the greatest war in history. The incumbent had been obliged to resign at the time of the Curragh Mutiny in the spring of 1914 and Asquith, as Prime Minister, had not thought it necessary to appoint a successor, keeping an eye on the War Office himself. Lord Kitchener was immediately appointed, a step the politicians were very soon to regret. At the first Cabinet meeting which he attended, he electrified his colleagues by telling them that, in his view, the war would last for at least three years and that he proposed to raise a force of seventy divisions, increasing the active army twelvefold. This he proceeded to do, asking for volunteers with the aid of one of the most famous posters of all time.

The response to Kitchener's call for volunteers has often been described. It was instantaneous and astounding; it grossly overwhelmed the military resources available, so that for many months men drilled with dummy weapons in the clothes in which they had enlisted, living in tented camps throughout the winter. By the end of September 750,000 men had joined the army, and eventually the total number of volunteers was 3,000,000. They were the finest army ever raised in Brit-

Francis Dodd, *Field-Marshal Viscount French of Ypres, KP, GCB, OM, GCVO, KCMG*
Charcoal and watercolour, 20 × 16¼ ins
Drawn in 1917, when French was Commander-in-Chief Home Forces. An emotional man of Irish descent, French had made his name as a cavalry commander before and during the Boer War. He had resigned as Chief of the Imperial General Staff in 1912 after the 'Curragh Mutiny', only to be appointed to command the British Expeditionary Force at the outbreak of the war; he was replaced by Haig in December 1915.

ain, the pick of the country – healthy, energetic, intelligent, patriotic, and burning to 'avenge Belgium'. For it was the Germans' cynical and opportunistic invasion of Belgium which was the crux in moving public opinion, rather than the obligations to France and to Russia, just as it had convinced the Cabinet that war would have to be declared. Men like H. H. Munro, alias the short-story writer 'Saki', who was then aged forty-four, and C. E. Montague, then forty-seven, falsified their ages in order to join up in the ranks of the army. Montague, later to write *Disenchantment*, one of the finest books of the period, was then a leader-writer on the *Manchester Guardian*, with a wife and seven children; he dyed his grey hair to lend verisimilitude to the deception.

Almost the whole country was swept up in patriotic enthusiasm and fervour, as tragic as it was admirable and doom-laden. There was, to a large extent, a romantic view of war. People, even many people in the army, supposed that the cavalry would charge at the enemy with lances and sabres*, exactly as had happened at Waterloo and in the Crimea. In the atmosphere that prevailed, it is not surprising that artists were swept up in this passionate outburst of national emotion. Like so many others, they wanted, as would have been said at the time, to 'do their bit'.

Mobilisation was very efficient in both Germany and France, less so in Russia. Germany had some 5,000,000 trained men to call on, France about 4,000,000. Germany was also very well prepared. The railway system of the country was admirably adapted to military needs; in the early days of August 1914 no less than 550 loaded troop trains crossed the Rhine bridges every day. The initial German strategy was to try to avoid the nation's perennial nightmare of a war on two fronts, that is against both Russia and France simultaneously. Correctly supposing that the Russian mobilisation would be protracted and incompetent, the plan was to hold the Eastern Front defensively while attacking France swiftly and decisively. The idea was to eliminate France first, and then turn Germany's full attention to the task of knocking out Russia. The Germans failed to achieve this in 1914. It was left to Hitler to demonstrate in 1940 how the first part of the process could be efficiently completed; but he too failed to achieve the second part, never succeeding in beating Russia in World War II.

The huge German wheeling movement through Belgium towards Paris, the Schlieffen Plan, went somewhat awry, partly because a tentative Russian invasion of East Prussia had rattled the German command into removing a couple of corps from the invasion of France to reinforce the eastern defences. While their north-eastern frontier was being invaded the French had meanwhile attacked the Germans in Lorraine, ineffectually and at a huge cost in casualties – they lost 300,000 men listed killed, wounded or missing, including 5,000 officers, in the first two weeks of the war.

As the Germans neared Paris, the politicians departed for Bordeaux. Although they reappeared later, their absence was fatal to the political control of the French army, which was scarcely regained: the French military headquarters, *Grand Quartier Général* (GQG), was largely supreme in France until 1918, when Clemenceau re-established political control.

* The future Field-Marshal Montgomery recalled that officers were obliged to get their swords sharpened on mobilisation, although they were never trained in their use, apart from ceremonial drill.

The British Expeditionary Force (BEF) of some five divisions, a mere 160,000 men, had taken its place on the French left flank, where it soon encountered at Mons the German army on its march through Belgium. From here the British were obliged to retreat, alongside the French, all the way back to the river Marne. At this point the German thrust faltered, its separate armies being insufficiently co-ordinated, and in turn the French and British were able to force the Germans to retreat back across the Aisne river. In the race towards the sea, in which both sides were trying to outflank each other, the advancing British transferred to Ypres.

It was at Ypres that the first substantial British battle took place, on land which was to become the graveyard of so many British soldiers in the next four years. It was here that the Germans were the first to demonstrate that frontal attacks, however bravely made, could not succeed against entrenched troops protected by barbed-wire entanglements and supported by well-sited machine-guns. On this occasion the British had poor trenches, no wire and few machine-guns. What they did have was the superb discipline and marksmanship of the old professional army, leading the Germans to suppose that far more machine-guns were available than was in fact the case. The Germans called this battle 'The Children's Massacre', since many young volunteer regiments were used in the frontal attacks. The British, more prosaically, called it First Ypres; British casualties in this battle totalled 54,000, one-third of the original BEF. It was the last battle of the old Regular Army. The German casualties on the Western Front in 1914 amounted to 1,000,000, and those of the French to nearly as many.

Late in 1914, as all the armies began to run short of ammunition, they dug themselves into the static lines of trenches which persisted on the Western Front, with minor adjustments, for the rest of the war. The trenches stretched all the way from the Swiss border to the sea; for most of this distance they were on French soil, except for the last few miles where the trenches were in Belgium. As it turned out, the Germans were far better equipped for trench warfare than the Allies. Their Maxim machine-guns were most effective, they were well supplied with mortars and howitzers which could lob shells right into the Allied trenches, and they had far more heavy artillery. Both the French and the British concentrated on lighter and more mobile guns, more suitable for the war of movement which had been envisaged.

It can be seen that the generals on both sides thought in the same way. For the British there was an additional problem, in that many of the senior general officers were cavalrymen who had made their military reputations in the wide open spaces of South Africa during the Boer War. They were now called upon to conduct siege warfare which, in effect, was what the fighting very largely amounted to on the Western Front. But being cavalry soldiers they thought in terms of dramatic breakthroughs when mobile forces, which were always held in readiness, would gallop through a breach in the enemy line. This was never to happen, and never *could* have happened, since the prolonged bombardments – often lasting a full week and still failing to destroy completely both those in the opposing trenches and dug-outs, and the protective barbed wire – always destroyed the communications

network and the roads along which the mobile forces might have advanced. Furthermore these officers, as horsemen, were especially hostile to the concept of using tanks when they began to be available to the British, albeit in crude form. Yet only the British had tanks and these machines could have conferred a crucial advantage. World War II was to demonstrate how very successful tanks could be when deployed against infantry in trenches, or in more elaborate defences.

Sir Muirhead Bone, *Tanks*
Charcoal, 21½ × 29½ ins
This dramatic drawing features a tank which has elements of both the Mark I and the Mark IV; it is symbolic rather than diagrammatic.

The volunteer army which Kitchener had raised had its first big test in September 1915, when the British attack at Loos was timed to coincide with French attacks in Artois and Champagne. Haig, then commanding the British First Army, remarked to the correspondent of *The Times* that 'As soon as we were supplied with ample artillery ammunition . . . we could walk through the German lines in several places'. This illusion was to cost scores of thousands of lives in due course. British casualties at Loos totalled 60,000, out of a total of 300,000 in the year. All the generals firmly believed the Napoleonic precept that vigorous attack, in sufficient strength and preceded by prolonged artillery bombardment, would always succeed. The failure at Loos was thought to be because the preliminary bombardment had been insufficient, or perhaps because the attacking troops had not been available in adequate numbers. The methods themselves were not questioned.

A memorable passage in C. S. Forester's study of the military mind of World War I, *The General*, describes a high-powered conference at which the Loos failure is analysed, yet the generals then set about planning an even larger battle to be fought on exactly the same lines. Forester's analogous illustration pictures a group of savages confronted for the first time with a screw, where previously only nails and pegs had been encountered. He describes how the first effort to pull out the screw had been fruitless, and how they set about devising larger systems of leverage, so that greater manpower could be brought into play. Their level of understanding simply did not allow them to contemplate the idea of turning instead of pulling, and they would have treated any suggestion of doing so with derisive laughter. *The General* is one of the best novels about the war, a tragic story brilliantly told with compelling irony.

On the Eastern, or Russian, Front the Germans had more than held their own, inflicting huge numbers of casualties on the ill-equipped Russian armies. Attempts to break the trench-bound deadlock were sought, usually by imaginative and over-optimistic politicians in the teeth of ferocious opposition from those military men who came to believe that the war could only be won on the Western Front. German colonies in west Africa and in South Africa had been subdued, but the east African colony of Tanganyika (now part of Tanzania) held out throughout the war. Totally unsupported, a handful of Germans with well-trained African troops successfully resisted far larger numbers of South African and British-led African and Indian troops for more than four years.

The entry of Turkey into the war on the German side, in November 1914, stimulated a number of ventures based on the erroneous supposition that attacks on Turkey would be a soft option, and the equally erroneous concept that a German collapse would inevitably follow the elimination of Turkey. The first of these ventures was the unsuccessful attempt by the Royal Navy to force the Dardanelles in the early months of 1915 and bombard the then Turkish capital of Constantinople, followed by the dramatic and very costly landings at Gallipoli.

The Anglo-French landing at Salonika in Macedonia in October 1915 was intended to stimulate resistance in the Balkans to German and Austrian forces. This it failed to do, Serbia being completely over-run by the Austrians. Nevertheless a force, eventually of 600,000 troops, a third of them British, manned the Salonika front for the rest of the war, haphazardly fighting the Bulgarian forces which had joined the Germans and Austrians in November 1915. The invasion of Turkish-held Mesopotamia (largely Iraq today) by British and Indian troops was not much more effective; it was originally designed with the limited object of protecting the Persian oilfields on which the Royal Navy depended for its supplies. A force of 300,000 was eventually engaged on this front.

The war at sea played an increasingly important part as the years of battle dragged on. In the early days, the Royal Navy had hunted down German surface raiders across the world; the Battle of the Falkland Islands was part of this far-flung effort. A blockade war ensued, of increasing ferocity and with increasing effect on both sides. The Anglo-French navies sought to stop all vessels from sailing to Germany or to Germany's allies. Neutral countries naturally resented this; but they resented Germany's counter-blockade to an even greater extent, as this involved the sinking by U-boats of shipping approaching the British Isles. Such ships, and sinkings, were numerous, since Britain was very heavily dependent on imports of both food and essential raw materials. Eventually, it was the German declaration of unrestricted U-boat warfare which pushed the USA into the war on the Allied side. This declaration, made in January 1917, meant that the Germans intended to sink all neutral shipping as the opportunity offered, without warnings.

Meanwhile, on 31 May 1916, the only great fleet action of the war had been fought. This was the Battle of Jutland, in which the German High Seas Fleet and the British Grand Fleet were engaged in strength, and which was an apparently inconclusive battle. Both sides confidently claimed a victory, although the British had lost twice as many ships and men as had the Germans. But the German fleet did not, in effect, again venture out into the North Sea; both sides glowered at each other from their respective harbours for the rest of the war.

Of course the existence of the German fleet, even in its harbours, forced the British to maintain their Grand Fleet in readiness when these ships might have been better employed elsewhere. But it was only after the end of the war that the German fleet eventually emerged, and then it sailed to Scapa Flow, first to surrender and then to scuttle the ships in a sort of mass naval suicide. It was a very strange end to the quarter-century of naval rivalry between the two nations, which had been conducted for years in a hysterical and jingoistic fashion.

On the Western Front, the conventional military thinking and planning resulted in the British attack which began on 1 July 1916, the Battle of the Somme. This was a greater calamity than Loos had been ten months earlier. The British now had fifty-seven divisions in France, thirteen of which climbed out of their trenches on 1 July to attack across no-man's-land. In the five months of battle, British casualties totalled 400,000; no fewer than 57,000 of these occurred on the first day of the struggle, and of that figure 19,000 were killed, a macabre and grisly record for the British army and, indeed, for any army in World War I.

February 1916 had seen the opening of the German attack on

Verdun. There was an especially sinister aspect to this attack, since the German strategists and planners did not even pretend to believe that the attacks would be successful and achieve the capture of the fortified town. Verdun was the lynchpin of the French defence system. The town had remained in French hands from the beginning, and was indeed to continue to do so. The German aim was attrition. They foresaw that the French would be compelled to defend the place at all costs; more and more troops would be sucked in to replace or boost the defenders; they believed that the French casualties would be greater than their own (they were in fact right about this, but only just); they also believed that French morale would be sapped and their will to fight eroded. In 1916 French casualties at Verdun exceeded 377,000, the

Sir Muirhead Bone, *A Cinema on Board a Battleship: HMS* Repulse
Black chalk, 15½ × 22 ins
Boredom had to be alleviated in the Grand Fleet, and a cinema show was one way of doing this. HMS *Repulse* was, in fact, a battle-cruiser; she was sunk off the Malayan coast (with HMS *Prince of Wales*) by the Japanese in December 1941.

Paul Nash, *After the Battle*
Pen and watercolour, 18¼ × 23½ ins
The littered aftermath of battle includes several corpses.

German casualties being some 40,000 fewer. As anticipated, almost every division in the French army was to spend a period of time in the Verdun defences. The Battle of the Somme had been fought partly as a response to this prolonged siege.

1916 saw the introduction of conscription in Britain; the miscarriage of another Russian attack; and Romania joined the Allies, only to be rapidly overrun by German forces. By this time it had been brought home to everyone – not only in Britain – that this war was an entirely different conflict from anything that had occurred throughout history. The huge loss of life, the vast numbers of wounded, the immense effort involved in the supply of munitions of all kinds, the increasing shortages of food, and the rationing of what food there was, not to speak of sporadic bombardment of coastal towns from raids by airships and aircraft, all helped to make people realise that this was a general, a total, war involving a total national effort. Evenly matched forces, at sea and on land, were caught in near-deadlock which could plainly last for a long time. But each failure and disappointment – and there were a large number of these – only reinforced the national determination to endure and to win in the end, and this did not happen only in Britain.

The casualty statistics, even today still capable of stunning the imagination, do not take account of the immensity of the human suffering, the heartwrenching anxieties, the burden of grief in countless homes, and the continuing suffering of the millions wounded by bullet or by shrapnel, poisoned by gas, or left with a permanent legacy of shellshock. People began to look upon the war as a vast and almost imper-

sonal calamity, apparently limitless in its appetite for human suffering. The most remarkable single fact to emerge from the war was, in the end, the astonishing capacity for human endurance which it revealed; and this occurred not only in the armed forces, and in the munition factories, but throughout the land.

The ruthless U-boat campaign which began in 1917 was initially highly effective. In February 540,000 tons of shipping approaching Britain was sunk, followed by 600,000 tons in March and 870,000 tons in April. The Germans had calculated that they would be able to starve Britain into submission with this campaign before the neutral Americans became sufficiently impatient to join the Allies. They came near to success, food stocks in Britain dwindling to a mere six weeks' worth by the end of April. But food rationing was tightened, anti-U-boat techniques were improved, and a convoy system was forced onto a reluctant Admiralty by Lloyd George, who was now Prime Minister; above all else, the USA joined the Allies in April. With its large merchant fleet, and its huge ship-building capacity, the situation was transformed.

But things had not gone well on land. Serious disaffection in the French army had led to mutinies in May and June 1917, and this was followed by a long period of stagnation in which it was thought inadvisable to use French troops in an attacking role. On the Western Front it was left to the British, under Haig, to keep up the pressure on the Germans. The consequence was the Battle of Passchendaele, by common consent amongst soldiers the most horrible of all the battles fought by the British throughout the war. Once again divisions trudged up to the

Sir Henry Rushbury, *Kensington Palace and Allotments*
Pencil, pen and watercolour, 11½ × 17¼ ins
An area of Kensington Gardens was given over to allotment gardens, as part of the campaign to grow as much food as possible in Britain and so reduce the amount which had to be imported.

James McBey, *Dawn, Camel Patrol Setting Out*
Etching, 9 × 15 ins
In desert areas the camel was used extensively as a beast of burden, and sometimes as a form of cavalry.

front line through the Menin Gate of Ypres. Months of fighting in mud and squalor resulted in 'gains' of not more than four miles, achieved at the cost of 400,000 casualties. The wettest August for many years added to the miseries of the troops in the flat landscape of Flanders, which had been churned into mud by the prolonged bombardment before the action began; heavily laden soldiers often drowned in the mud.

The only gleams of success came from the Middle East, where Baghdad had been reached in March, and where Allenby's imaginatively conceived attacks on the Turks had led to the occupation of Jerusalem in December – his forces, originally withdrawn from Gallipoli and defending the Suez Canal, had now swollen to 500,000 men from Britain and the dominions.

The Germans believed that they still had one chance of success. The Russian Revolution of 1917 rapidly led to Russia suing for peace.

Freed, therefore, of their Eastern Front, the Germans were able to concentrate on a huge last effort in France, believing that they could achieve success before American forces could be mustered there in sufficient numbers to make a decisive contribution. The Germans struck in March 1918, attacking on the front of the British Fifth Army, at the point where it was alongside the northernmost French troops. Yet again they came near to success, driving forward with great skill and energy, almost forcing a wedge between the British and French armies, reaching the Marne again and getting within forty miles of Paris. But, once more, desperate defence was triumphant, and at last the turning point had been reached. The crisis also forced a Supreme Commander, Foch, onto the Allies for the first time.

After years of losses and of suffering the effects of blockade, the Germans were becoming demoralised. The British and, increasingly, the Americans, now with more than thirty divisions, were able to fight a series of successful battles from August 1918 onwards. As in the earliest days, a war of movement was fought. Successful attacks, moreover, were not pressed forward unremittingly – once success was achieved, the troops stayed in their new positions while further attacks were launched elsewhere, as tanks and artillery were now used more effectively. The Germans were forced to retreat, but the end came before they reached their own frontiers. Some of their forces began to mutiny, the Kaiser abdicated and fled to Holland, a republic was declared in Berlin; and the generals, the effective rulers of Germany since 1914, sought peace.

The British Empire, as it then was, had lost almost 1,000,000 men killed, of whom 744,000 came from the United Kingdom. Something like three times as many men were wounded or injured in some way. The human suffering had been on an unimaginable scale.

Wyndham Lewis, *A Battery Position in a Wood*
Pen and watercolour, 12½ × 18½ ins
Camouflaged howitzers, the forward ammunition dump and living quarters in a dug-out are to be seen, with a homely washing line. An empty shell-case hangs ready for use as a warning gong in the event of a gas attack.

THE ARTISTS AT WAR

Many artists enlisted in the first days of the war, and not only the younger ones. For these men the Artists' Rifles was clearly an attractive unit to join; it was originally a Volunteer regiment, largely supported by artists, and its ranks were swollen at this time by C. S. Jagger (then aged twenty-nine) and the Nash brothers, Paul (twenty-five) and John (twenty-one), amongst others. Even Lavery, aged fifty-eight, joined and drilled for a while in the courtyard of Burlington House, but his quixotic gesture came to a rapid end with ill-health forcing his retirement. Wyndham Lewis (thirty-two) and Colin Gill (twenty-two) joined the artillery. And in 1915 the Royal Army Medical Corps accepted the Spencer brothers, Stanley (twenty-four) and Gilbert (a year younger).

In some cases artists had additional reasons for enlisting, besides the general patriotic motives shared by so many hundred of thousands of others. Unsurprisingly, the outbreak of war saw the immediate collapse of the art market, causing real difficulties for many – especially the younger, yet-to-be-established artists. Also, for some, no doubt the emotional stimulus of war was an element in the decision to join.

Many of these enthusiasts were indeed stimulated, and were able to produce pictures reflecting their experiences. When these started to appear in London exhibitions they had great popular success. This led to agitation for the appointment of official war artists. Influential personages such as Sir William Rothenstein, Lady Cunard and Philip Sassoon led the pressure group, as it would later have been called. There was nothing new in the concept of officially appointed artists being used to record warfare. Such appointments had been made, usually in connection with war at sea, since the late seventeenth century when the émigré Dutch marine artists, Willem van der Velde, father and son, both sailed with the Royal Navy.

But in fact the first war artists were appointed to serve the needs of propaganda – the business of presenting the British war effort to best effect, especially towards neutral countries, either to keep them neutral, to make them into friendly neutrals or, better still, to persuade them to join the Allies. The main propaganda target was, of course, the United States, a neutral power, isolationist by long tradition, but fortunately English-speaking.

The Cabinet was sharply aware of the need for propaganda. It had had the greatest difficulty in taking the decision to go to war on 4 August, and if Belgium had not been invaded, it might never have so persuaded itself; as it was, one Cabinet minister did indeed resign. Perhaps that long process of self-persuasion, which had racked it for days on end, also caused it to realise that much effort would be needed to convince neutral countries of the need to remain neutral or to become friendly. It no doubt recalled, too, how unpopular Britain had become across the world during the Boer War. Many nations became hostile, if not actively so, during this conflict, with no effort being made to persuade them otherwise. The Cabinet secretly established a propaganda department as early as August 1914.

This was done in a haphazard but effective manner. C. F. G. Masterman, then both Chancellor of the Duchy of Lancaster and chairman of the recently formed National Health Insurance Commission, was invited to create a propaganda department. This started work in the Commission's offices and became known by the name of those offices, Wellington House. Secret activity was therefore accidentally provided with a ready-made cover story.

Masterman, born in 1874, was an intriguing person. After a brilliant Cambridge career, he had a meteoric start in journalism. He illuminated the changing social conditions of Britain with an engaging mixture of apprehension, nostalgia and Christian Socialist sympathy; his best-known book is *The Condition of England*, published in 1909. His first appointment was as Under-Secretary at the Home Office, when Churchill was in charge of the department. In 1912 he was advanced to the most important of all under-secretaryships, Financial Secretary to the Treasury. In February 1914 he was appointed Chancellor of the Duchy of Lancaster, then a Cabinet post.

This was a disaster for him. In those days appointment to head a department of state, which is what the duchy was in theory, involved holding a by-election whereby the newly appointed minister was, as it were, confirmed as an MP. Masterman had the embarrassing misfortune to fail to be re-elected; embarrassment turned to something worse when he failed again at another by-election elsewhere. He went on trying to find a 'safe' seat which would have him, his position getting more and more anomalous, but he never succeeded, and was obliged to resign from the Cabinet in February 1915. His political career was over. He was still a Cabinet minister in August 1914, however, and he still had some power and influence, although this was dwindling week by week; and he was close to Lloyd George, with whom he had worked at the Treasury.

Masterman rapidly built up a staff of amateur civil servants at Wellington House. These included, at one time or another, Arnold Toynbee, the future author of *A Study of History*; Arthur Conan Doyle, all of whose Sherlock Holmes stories had by now been published; and John Buchan, whose first adventure story, *The Thirty-Nine Steps*, was to be published in 1915. But literary men did not have a monopoly. The staff included Eric Maclagan, later to become Director of the Victoria and Albert Museum; Campbell Dodgson, Keeper of Prints and Drawings at the British Museum; Thomas Derrick, an artist and a teacher at the Royal College of Art; and Alfred Yockney, the former editor of *Art Journal*.

Words could readily be poured out in the magazines, news-sheets and books which Wellington House started to produce, in ever-increasing numbers, for distribution across the world. But it was soon found that words were not enough. Pictures were needed, both to enliven the text and, where possible, to create memorable images. The photographs which came back from France were few in number and often poor in quality. The flat countryside of northern France, the nature of trench warfare and the cumbersome cameras of the day were of no help to the photographers. Nor did the activities of the military censors help greatly – they had rigid rules, such as that which forbade at all costs any picture which included the dead body of a British soldier.

Pictures were an urgent necessity. It would, of course, have been possible to make use of cartoonists: Bruce Bairnsfather's 'Old Bill' was already well known. Equally it would have been possible to make use of illustrators – Thomas Derrick was a distinguished book illustrator. But Masterman himself decided that artists should be used. His understanding of the government machinery meant that he could find ways to overcome the inevitable obstacles, arranging funding to pay the artists' salaries as well as persuading the War Office to facilitate the artists' work, arrange transport, and generally deal with the required logistics.

MUIRHEAD BONE was the first official artist to be sent to France.

He had been born into a talented family in Glasgow – his brother David became a distinguished master mariner and writer, while his brother James was a journalist of some significance, eventually becoming the London editor of the *Manchester Guardian*. Muirhead Bone was apprenticed to a Glasgow architect but never practised as such, preferring to work as an etcher and watercolour artist, usually of topographical subjects. He established a high reputation for himself, and has been described as 'the greatest virtuoso of architectural drawing since Piranesi'.

This judgement suggests, quite correctly, that Muirhead Bone's work was in the classical tradition. But Bone was not a hidebound aca-

Sir Muirhead Bone, *Men of the RFC Building their Winter Huts, near Albert*
Black chalk and watercolour, 7½ × 12¼ ins
The Nissen Hut, here shown under construction, was a familiar structure in both
World Wars, made from tunnel-shaped corrugated iron mounted on concrete. It
was named after its inventor, Lt-Col Peter Nissen.

demic artist. He had lived and worked in both France and Italy, and he
had an open-minded disposition. He was a close friend of Jacob
Epstein with whom, one would have supposed, he had little in common artistically. He earned a good deal in his chosen field, and was a
generous patron of other artists. In later years he was to recognise at
once the high talents of such artists as Graham Sutherland and Henry
Moore, artists who were to work in a very different tradition. He was a
quick worker, and a warm-hearted, honest and unselfish man.*

* I met Bone briefly once or twice in 1949, when I was working for Basil
Blackwell in Oxford where Bone then lived. Blackwell, himself always known as
'The Gaffer', was an ardent dispenser of nicknames; he always referred to Bone,
rather unkindly, as 'Sir Muddlehead'. I forget now why Bone used to appear in
Broad Street; no doubt some book was in preparation.

Sir Muirhead Bone, *The Great Crater, Athies*
Charcoal, 22 × 30 ins
Athies, two or three miles to the east of Arras, in France, was taken by the British
in April 1917, not long before Bone recorded the scene.

The term 'old boy network' might well have been invented for Wellington House. Bone, then aged forty, was recruited in May 1916 by his
friend A. P. Watt, the literary agent, who was yet another man from the
world of books on the staff at Wellington House. This was thought to
be altogether a wise suggestion in view of Bone's well-known skill in
depicting ruins, of which there were many in France by 1916. Commissioned as an honorary second lieutenant, he reached France in August.
This was some six weeks after the opening of the Battle of the Somme,
the long-drawn-out holocaust in which Kitchener's volunteer army was
slaughtered in staggering numbers. Bone toured the enormous battlefield, working hard – by early October he had sent home to London
some 150 finished drawings. But he complained that the ruins he

had seen were too ruinous, too flattened to make effective pictures.

Bone returned to London and did further work in munitions factories, and with the Grand Fleet. He returned to France in 1917, and then found that the German withdrawal to the Hindenburg Line had provided him with access to innumerable ruined towns and villages, which he portrayed assiduously. Back home again he had a spell in his native Glasgow, working in the shipyards, and then had a further stint with the Royal Navy. At this point, after working so hard for so long, he had a kind of breakdown. Meanwhile his energy and generous enthusiasm for the work of other artists did much to help create the fine art collection of the Imperial War Museum.

His post-war career carried on very much where he had left off. Knighted in 1937, he was to be the doyen of war artists in World War II, working entirely with the navy until he retired in 1943.

Bone's drawings vary from swift thumbnail sketches to large architectural compositions, detailed with great mastery. The guns and tanks, and the destruction which they caused, are all recorded in sober, unemotional and detached detail, often arranged with the greatest possible dramatic effect. But Bone's war, or his vision of war, seems dry and factual, muted but precise.

Muirhead Bone was a man who knew his own limitations. He perceived himself, rightly or wrongly, as lacking skill as a portraitist. Therefore he was quick to recommend another artist when Masterman, needing an expert in producing portraits rapidly and effectively, made enquiries. The need arose from pressure on Masterman to 'boom' (in the current slang) British admirals, generals and other leading figures in the war effort, publicising them to the world. Bone's suggested portraitist was another etcher and painter, two years his senior and his own brother-in-law, FRANCIS DODD.

Francis Dodd also shared with Bone a Glasgow upbringing and a straightforward classical style. Son of a Wesleyan minister, he had trained at Glasgow School of Art, in Paris and in Italy. While not in the front rank of portrait painters as, for example, were Orpen and de László, he was well regarded; he had been a member of the Royal Society of Portrait Painters since 1911. To the experts at Wellington House, it was a great advantage that he was able to work well in charcoal and watercolour. It was thought that he would be able to use this technique better than oils in the conditions which he was likely to encounter – surely rather a naïve judgement, since senior generals inhabited châteaux and were notorious for never visiting the forward areas. It was also thought that reproduction of charcoal drawings would present fewer technical difficulties than reproduction of oil paintings.

Initially Dodd spent eight weeks in France, producing more than thirty portraits of general officers, as well as others whom he met at the various headquarters he visited. He did more on his return to London, in some cases creating from photographs the portraits of those whom he had been unable to see. Then he moved on, to produce many por-

Francis Dodd, *General Sir William Robertson, GCB, KCVO, DSO*
Charcoal and watercolour, 10½ × 9½ ins
Drawn in January 1918 when this remarkable man was Chief of the Imperial General Staff. He had served in the ranks for ten years before being commissioned, then augmenting his meagre pay by gaining qualifications in no less than six languages. Intelligence posts led to his appointment as commandant of the Staff College in 1910. He was CIGS from 1915 to 1918.

traits of admirals. Eventually, however, he ran out of enthusiasm for this kind of war work.

Dodd was a large, placid man. He had had great trouble with his military uniform when he first went to France, and had been heard to remark that he wished that Colonel Sam Browne, the inventor of the officer's leather belt, had never lived. His post-war life was relatively uneventful. He became a trustee of the Tate Gallery in 1929 – this was in the midst of a period when two successive directors of that institution were doing their best to ensure that no Post-Impressionist pictures were ever hung on the walls of the Tate, a policy which Dodd must have accepted. He became an RA in 1935, and died at his Blackheath home in 1949.

Wellington House was not the only propaganda agency at work. There were others, all of them under the vague control of the Foreign Office. The War Office was unhappy about many of the multifarious activities of these unintegrated organisations. The War Office had also learnt to understand something of the mercurial mind of Lloyd George during the relatively short time he had been in charge as War Minister (July to December 1916). No time was wasted: Lloyd George had not been Prime Minister for much more than a week before a measured protest was made.

More than any other minister, Lloyd George had a natural understanding of propaganda. He was a master of personal promotion and was on close terms with many newspaper editors. He now asked one of these, Robert Donald of the *Daily Chronicle* which was then a national daily, to investigate the problem and make suggestions. This was duly and quickly done. Donald recommended grouping all the propaganda agencies in a single Department of Information, separate from all other departments or ministries. This department was established in February 1917 and had its own funds.

John Buchan was chosen to head it. He had worked briefly at Wellington House and had then moved to an Intelligence post at the Foreign Office, where he held the rank of lieutenant-colonel. In earlier days he had been one of Alfred Milner's young men in South Africa, where he had become a friend of Haig, now the Commander-in-Chief in France. Milner was now a member of the War Cabinet, so Buchan had friends at court on both sides of the Channel. His new department had four sections and one of these, the Literary and Art Section, was Masterman's Wellington House operation.

One of the immediate results of the establishment of the Department of Information was a response to an outstanding request for an artist from General Murray, the Commander-in-Chief in the Middle East, based in Cairo.

Campbell Dodgson's nomination for this post was an inspired one – he suggested JAMES McBEY. McBey's story was extraordinary. He was born in 1883 near Aberdeen, and was educated at a village school. The first ten years of his working life were gruesome, spent as a bank clerk in Aberdeen, grinding away at the dullest possible job and being the sole support of his widowed mother and his grandmother. All this time he nursed a passionate determination to become an artist. He went to such evening classes as were available; he read the whole of the art section of the Aberdeen Public Library; he taught himself, slowly and painfully, the skills of his trade. He produced his first etching, a technique at which he was to excel, by adapting his mother's mangle as an etching press.

By 1910 he had managed to scrape together £200. With this, he took the tremendous risk of leaving his job, spending some of the money on a trip to Holland to study Rembrandt's landscapes. The following year saw his work first exhibited in London, with immediate success. A visit

to Morocco in 1912 led on to some admirable watercolours. By 1914 his reputation was not so very different from that of Muirhead Bone. His craftsmanship was admirable, his technique brisk and unfussy.

It was the Morocco experience, together with McBey's obvious and wholly admirable determination, which rightly brought him to Dodgson's mind. McBey had enlisted and at that time was employed as a second lieutenant in the army's printing establishment in Rouen. He was extracted from this post and sent off to Cairo.

By the time he reached Egypt the plodding Murray had been replaced by the immensely dynamic and imaginative General Allenby. McBey travelled with Allenby's army, from the Suez Canal across the Sinai desert to Palestine and eventually on into Syria, an exhilarating campaign in which cavalry was used frequently and effectively, almost the last time in the history of warfare that this was to happen. McBey witnessed and recorded Allenby's entry into Jerusalem in December 1917.

McBey was greatly hampered by transport difficulties, as well as all the natural problems caused by flies, heat, sandstorms and fever. But in his quiet, unfussy and determined way, he triumphantly overcame all impediments and his output was prodigious – nearly 300 drawings, watercolours and oils sent home in well under two years. His work had great style and grace. Some of it took the form of portraits, and his subjects included T. E. Lawrence, the Emir Feisal and other Arab leaders who operated on Allenby's right flank; but McBey was never able to move and work with these romantic figures.

Returning to London, McBey quietly picked up his career where he had left it. His etchings, many of them derived from his wartime work, sold well and he prospered in the 1920s. Marrying an American, Marguerite Loeb, in 1931, he became an American citizen himself during World War II. Later he lived in Tangier, where he died in 1959.

As soon as the Department of Information had come into being, the Literary and Art Section had at once arranged for two Irish artists to visit France. One of these was the very successful portrait painter WILLIAM ORPEN, who in the public eye had succeeded Sargent as the most fashionable portraitist in London, just as Sargent had in his day succeeded Millais.

Orpen, twenty years younger than Sargent, was born in 1878, the fourth son of a Protestant Dublin solicitor, a skilful Sunday painter in watercolour. He does not seem to have had much formal schooling, in spite of his reasonably affluent background. But he evidently knew exactly what he wanted to do with his life, going to art school in his native city before moving on to the Slade School. This was a golden period in the history of the Slade, with Augustus John, Wyndham Lewis and Ambrose McEvoy all students there with Orpen; but the Irishman, not much more than five feet in height, was a splendid draughtsman with fanatical determination, possibly powered by his lack of inches. He was well able to keep his end up in this talented company.

James McBey, *The Allies Entering Jerusalem, 11 December 1917*
Oil, 42 × 60 ins
The massive figure of General Allenby, whose army nickname was 'The Bull', is flanked by representatives of the French and the Italians, both countries having detachments serving in Allenby's force.

He was hungry for knowledge – knowledge, that is, about art. He studied the masters of the past with enthusiasm, and had great skill in adapting the techniques of the past into his own idiom. He made his name very early with two well-known pictures: *The Play Scene from Hamlet*, painted when he was still a Slade student, and *The Mirror*, painted in 1900.

He married Grace Knewstub the following year, thus becoming William Rothenstein's brother-in-law. For a short while he and his former fellow-student Augustus John jointly ran a teaching studio in Chelsea. But this could not last, John's ultra-Bohemian approach to life contrasting totally with Orpen's hard efficiency, drive and ambition, although these qualities were masked by Irish charm, by wit and by an easy conviviality. Orpen soon became known for his portraits of public figures – he was to paint more than 600 in his fifty-three years. These portraits were strong in colour, assured in draughtsmanship, with many well-observed details; they had a highly polished style, almost harsh, which set a pattern for Academicians' boardroom exactitude for several generations.

Sometimes he achieved great distinction, as with his well-known group portrait *Hommage à Manet*, painted in 1909 and showing a gathering of friends at Sir Hugh Lane's house in South Bolton Gardens, which Orpen himself was to own in later years. Becoming an Associate Royal Academician (ARA) in 1910, he was already something of an Establishment figure. The following year he became a founder-member of the National Portrait Society. Later, he painted a magnificent portrait of Churchill. This was in 1916, when the statesman was out of office and deeply unhappy. Orpen conveyed in masterly fashion both Churchill's desperate frustration and his indomitable courage, and the picture was to become the great man's favourite portrait.*

Orpen joined the army in 1916. He moved effortlessly into the easiest of circumstances, his friend the Quartermaster General, Sir John Cowans, arranging for him a commission in the Army Service Corps and a 'cushy billet', as the current slang had it, in Kensington Barracks. Theoretically in the army, he nevertheless contrived to earn £7,000 and more from portrait painting that year; this work, of course, included the Churchill portrait, which was a gift from Lord Rothermere. Orpen was supremely well connected: Lord Derby, who became War Minister in December 1916, had sat for him; he knew Haig; and he knew Haig's private secretary, Philip Sassoon.

Orpen jumped at the chance of going to France, offered to him by the Department of Information. He was sent on a trip which was to last three weeks. But something altogether extraordinary happened: Orpen stayed in France for three years.

Shamelessly exploiting his highly placed connections, Orpen became more or less a law unto himself. He not only had a car and a driver, as well as a batman, but he also acquired a sort of manager, an army captain who dealt with all the logistical details. After a while he added a mistress to his entourage. Orpen himself had been promoted overnight from second lieutenant to major.

He certainly enjoyed himself enormously. He travelled all over the British sector. He would move from the Hôtel de la Paix in Amiens to Paris for a few days, then back to the Hôtel Sauvage at Cassel. He was a familiar figure at all the headquarters, where his high spirits and jolly manner were always welcome. He shrewdly kept all uncomfortable questions at bay by paying for everything out of his own, admittedly capacious, pocket.

He was appalled and fascinated in equal measure by everything he

* I was very fortunate to see this splendid picture on several occasions when professional duties took me to Randolph Churchill's house at East Bergholt; the portrait is unforgettable.

Sir William Orpen, *Field-Marshal Sir Douglas Haig, KT, GCB, GCVO, KCIE*
Oil, 29½ × 25 ins
This dashing portrait dates from 30 May 1917, at GHQ at Montreuil. Haig had commanded 1st Corps in 1914, then 1st Army; he succeeded French as Commander-in-Chief in December 1915.

saw. But was this fascination the only thing that kept him there? He had freedom in France, or rather he had organised his own unique form of freedom; and perhaps he did not feel as free in London. Had he begun to tire of the treadmill of fashionable portraiture, as Sargent did? This has to be a possibility, so that his brilliant self-portrait *Ready to Start* (page 29) might well record, for the artist, a new beginning.

While certainly appalled by all that he saw, as is clear from his own account of those years *An Onlooker in France*, he was usually content to record everything with characteristic industry and skill – but coldly, even clinically, and unemotionally, rather than introducing any note of comment. His drawings are always decorative, but rarely more than

Sir William Orpen, *Some Members of the Allied Press Camp, with their Press Officers*
Oil, 36 × 30 ins
This group portrait of uniformed war correspondents conveys a sense of Orpen's enjoyment of his quasi-military status; also, perhaps, some of the frustrations of journalists working under strict control and censorship.

Sir William Orpen, *Dead Germans in a Trench*
Oil, 36 × 30 ins
The military censors never objected to enemy casualties in pictures. German trenches were often made with great care, skilfully revetted, as here, and sometimes making lavish use of concrete.

that, although there are exceptions, such as *Dead Germans in a Trench*. And by his own standards, his portraits from these war years are not very distinguished; amongst many others, he painted portraits of Haig, Trenchard, Plumer, Foch and Seely.

Orpen was not a deep-thinking man. Accounts of him all refer to his amazing ignorance of the world and its affairs, apart from art; he always joked that he had been brought up on the Irish Question, but had never discovered what the question was. He loved his work and he loved games, particularly table tennis, and was not in the least interested in anything else. But this ebullient man came to develop enormous

Sir William Orpen, *Ready to Start*
Oil, 24 × 20 ins
A self-portrait, dated Cassel, 10 June 1917. Cassel, twenty miles south of Dunkirk, was always in Allied hands. Something of Orpen's comfortable lifestyle is evident; but a sheepskin jerkin is perhaps excessive in June.

Sir William Orpen, *The Signing of the Peace in the Hall of Mirrors, Versailles, 28 June 1919*
Oil, 60 × 50 ins
Wilson, Clemenceau and Lloyd George are the central figures in this group portrait. The large cast of characters includes Sir Maurice Hankey, A. J. Balfour and the Maharajah of Bikaner. But the statesmen seem to be dwarfed by their surroundings. Had the artist begun to see them as pygmies?

Sir William Orpen, *To the Unknown British Soldier in France*
Oil, 60 × 50½ ins
The origin of this strange picture is described on page 32. It was painted before the tomb of the Unknown Warrior was installed in Westminster Abbey on 11 November 1920.

Sir William Orpen, *Harvest, 1918*
Oil, 30 × 25 ins
An anguished and not wholly successful attempt by the artist to underline the tragedy of war. Orpen presented the picture to the Imperial War Museum in 1930.

respect and affection for the ordinary soldier. He came to understand, and was amazed by, the stoic, humorous fortitude of the men in the trenches. He admired without any reservations their resilience, their powers of endurance, their good-natured tolerance and the comradeship amongst them.

It was this intense feeling which led to the strangest episode in Orpen's life. He was at the peace conference at Versailles, commissioned by the government to record the event for posterity. This he duly did, with two pictures which must have conformed, more or less, to what Lloyd George and his colleagues expected. These are *A Peace*

Conference at the Quai d'Orsay and *The Signing of the Peace in the Hall of Mirrors, Versailles*. But it is possible that there is an element of irony in these pictures, with the huge scale of the rooms overwhelming the politicians, so that they seem almost pygmies.

Orpen painted a third group portrait of the participants. But he became disgusted by the petty greed and cynicism of the Allied politicians, which contrasted so sharply with the generous nature of the men he had encountered in the trenches. He could not get out of his mind the millions of dead, the maimed, the gassed, the wounded, and those driven out of their minds. He painted out thirty or forty small portraits and replaced them instead with a single covered catafalque, calling his picture *To the Unknown British Soldier in France*. When the picture was first exhibited in London, the draped coffin was flanked by two ghostly figures of soldiers standing guard, incongruously topped by putti. There was a public outcry and the picture was altered, the guards and the putti also being painted out.

Orpen's gesture, made with the best of intentions, fell flat. He desperately wanted to say something, but comment of any kind was foreign to his nature and he lacked the painterly qualities to translate his protest into a coherent message. But he should be honoured for trying.

Knighted in 1918, becoming an RA the next year, Orpen returned to his pre-war life with frenetic relish. Artistically he slipped downhill, his portraits in the 1920s moving from the undistinguished to the commonplace, and from the commonplace to the shamelessly vulgar. Perhaps he never recovered from the spiritual upheaval he had experienced at Versailles in 1919. He died in 1931.

It had been arranged that JOHN LAVERY would go to France at the same time as Orpen. They were the two most famous and popular portrait painters in Britain in the immediate pre-war years. The generals in France must have been flattered to think that they were to sit to these paragons, both of them extremely well known, especially in the London social world.

But Lavery did not, in fact, go to France. Very prudently, he had prepared a motor-van in which he proposed living. Unfortunately he and his wife had a bad crash in this vehicle in the London blackout, a restriction imposed because Zeppelin bombing raids were an occasional hazard. Both suffered concussion in the crash, and then had a type of breakdown. Lavery's visit to France was first postponed and then abandoned.

While not in any sense an innovatory painter, Lavery was certainly a remarkable man. He was born in Belfast in 1856, in thoroughly unpromising circumstances. His father was a failure as a publican,

Sir John Lavery, *A Convoy, North Sea, 1918*
Oil, 68 × 78 ins
Painted from an airship (N7) only a few weeks before the Armistice, Lavery's exciting picture shows a convoy of merchant vessels off the Norwegian coast.

Sir John Lavery, *The Cemetery, Étaples, 1919*
Oil, 23½ × 36 ins
Some British military hospitals were sited at Etaples (known to soldiers as 'Eat-apples'), some fifteen miles south of Boulogne, on the main railway line to Paris. Lavery painted this scene in 1919, before the Imperial War Graves Commission had begun their work of establishing the well-tended cemeteries which are scattered all across north-eastern France.

Sir John Lavery, *Army Post Office 3, Boulogne, 1919*
Oil, 40 × 50 ins
Elaborate arrangements were in place from the early days of trench warfare on the Western Front, for mail both to and from the troops in France. By the date of Lavery's picture, almost all the staff were female.

surely a bizarre achievement in that hard-drinking city. Seeking a new start in life, he emigrated to America in 1859, only to be drowned at sea when his ship sank in mid-Atlantic. Lavery's mother died of grief, leaving her three-year-old son to be brought up in harsh conditions by relatives in Ulster and in Ayrshire. In neither place was he able to achieve much in the way of formal education.

Escape of a kind was achieved in 1873, when Lavery was apprenticed to a Glasgow painter/photographer; he also attended Glasgow School of Art. His natural talents were such that he was able to establish himself as an artist in Glasgow in 1879. He studied further in London, and in Paris in 1881–2.

Lavery was most influenced by Bastien-Lepage and by Whistler. The latter's influence was also felt by many of the young and lively members of the Glasgow School, a loose association of young artists which began to coalesce around 1880. Lavery was involved with this group, which became widely known in Britain, Germany and America, especially in the 1890s. Pictures of the Glasgow School can be said to be characterised by strength, by the absence of any sort of narrative content, and by internationalism.

Lavery first exhibited in London, at the Royal Academy, in 1886, and moved permanently to London at the turn of the century. He had a fondness for genre pictures, but he had great commercial success as a portrait painter. His group portrait of the royal family in Buckingham Palace, now in the National Portrait Gallery, is a fine example of his style. This was essentially traditional. He was said to paint in the manner of Velázquez, with a perfunctory acknowledgement to Impressionism in his highly toned colours and his rapid brushwork.

He used to say that his success was largely due to the social qualities of his American second wife, Hazel. But this was over-modest: he was a flamboyant Ulsterman of great talent and industry.

After his French visit had aborted, the Department of Information sent him touring around the home front, as it was now called. He spent some time with the navy, in the Firth of Forth and elsewhere; he went to many munitions works, in Newcastle, in Edinburgh and in Elizabethville, a brand-new village entirely devoted to the making of shells and peopled exclusively by Belgian refugees. Lavery was one of the first artists to take as a subject aspects of the war in the air – aeroplanes at Hendon, airships at Roehampton, kite-balloons; he also recorded the eventual surrender of the German fleet in *The End*, a group portrait of the surrender ceremony, dominated by Admiral Beatty. But most of the portraits he painted as a war artist were in sharp contrast to the 'society' portraits of his pre-war years, being of deckhands, female shipbuilders and skippers of minesweepers.

Lavery took little interest in politics, even Irish politics. In spite of his gesture of enlisting in August 1914, he was pacifist in outlook; he was known in artistic circles in Germany. His emotions were not violently engaged and, in any event, he was never able to get close to the real horrors of war, especially those of the trenches. His wartime pictures, splendidly painted for the most part, seem muted, lacking in passion, almost uninterested. He himself thought that they were 'as dull as ditchwater'.

Knighted in 1918, he became an RA three years later – for some reason he had been out of favour at the Academy in pre-war years. He carried on much as before. One of the pictures he sent to the Academy for the Summer Exhibition of 1940, the year before he died, was dutifully reproduced. It looked astonishingly old-fashioned, a Victorian relic, painted in the style which had served him so well for sixty years.

When it became clear that John Lavery was not able to go to France, it was urgently necessary to find a replacement. Permission had been given for two artists to go, and the Department of Information was keen to take up this concession in case it might later be revoked. Up to this time, the artists sent across the Channel had been traditional in outlook and style; they were unlikely to cause any sort of distress to high-ranking military personages or to bewilder any censor. The choice now fell on a completely different breed of artist, a much younger man, one of the small handful of British artists who had actually been involved in the immediate pre-war artistic ferment described earlier, and the only self-styled English Futurist. How this violent U-turn in policy came about is not without interest.

CHRISTOPHER RICHARD WYNNE NEVINSON, normally known as C. R. W. Nevinson, was a natural rebel, born in 1889. His father, H. W. Nevinson, was a celebrated journalist and war correspondent, and was indeed best known in the latter role in spite of being a fierce and articulate pacifist. His mother similarly combined activity in the women's suffrage campaign, pressure for Poor Law relief, and other causes with jingoistic views on many subjects. Unpopular causes were the daily small change of these Hampstead intellectuals, violent discussion and argument their daily bread: they were uncomfortable parents.

Nevinson, who always seems to have felt at odds with the world, and who later developed persecution mania, used to claim that his parents' radical views meant that he himself was booed on the streets of Hampstead as a child. If true, this would certainly have contributed to his permanent sense of ill-usage by the world at large.

Nevinson *père* combined radical views with a firm belief in the virtues of a traditional classical education, and nursed a desire that eventually his son would follow him to Balliol. He sent C.R.W. to Uppingham with this end in view. Poor health was to pursue the younger Nevinson throughout his life, and it intervened now to release him from uncongenial public-school life. In convalescence he visited the Continent with his mother; as it happened, she was not without knowledge and understanding of art, including the modern art which was then to be seen in Paris. Nevinson began to draw.

C. R. W. Nevinson, *The Road from Arras to Bapaume*
Oil, 24 × 18 ins
Something of the atmosphere of this picture can be experienced in a drive down the N17. Not unnaturally, the British army had to adopt the French practice of driving on the right-hand side of the road.

C. R. W. Nevinson, *A Taube*
Oil, 25 × 30 ins
Taubes, made either by Kondor or by Jeannin, were normally used in the earlier days of the war for scouting and for observation, and not, as shown here, for attacking civilian targets. *Taube* is German for pigeon, or dove.

In 1907 he went to the St John's Wood School of Art. He reacted against the academic training of this institution and transferred to the Slade School. While a student he started to make a modest name for himself, chiefly with townscapes in the Impressionist manner. He was given some encouragement by Sickert, Gilman and Gore, the leading painters of the Camden Town School, with which Nevinson began to form some tentative links. But at this time Henry Tonks, the imperious teacher at the Slade, told Nevinson that he lacked sufficient talent to become a painter and that he ought to give it up. Naturally this devastated Nevinson. For a brief while he did give up, trying Fleet Street instead. He was not to know that Tonks had, even more fatuously, said the same thing to Matthew Smith a few years earlier.

Fortunately Fleet Street was not a success. The despirited Nevinson took himself off to Paris, to the Académie Julian. This was in 1911, and he plunged with relish into the welter of artistic excitements of the city.

C. R. W. Nevinson, *The Harvest of Battle*
Oil, 72 × 125 ins
The grim and desolate scene depicted in this large canvas, painted in 1919 in a more traditional style than much of Nevinson's earlier work, reflects the depth of the artist's feeling about the destruction around him.

He felt and absorbed the full impact of Cubism; he shared a studio with Modigliani; he met Marinetti. The latter encounter led to his adopting the Futurist style, the only British artist to follow this creed, with its doctrine of beauty found in modern machinery and its slogans about beauty in strife and in aggressiveness.

When war came Nevinson joined the Red Cross, something which no doubt satisfied his mother's patriotic instincts while not offending his father's pacifist principles. At first he was sent to Dunkirk, where the French medical services had collapsed under the strain of the enormous demands being made on them. The scenes which Nevinson encountered as a driver, interpreter, stretcher-bearer and hospital orderly were harrowing almost beyond belief and were never to leave him throughout his life, remaining hauntingly vivid and appalling. Presently he joined the Royal Army Medical Corps, where he met almost equally harrowing scenes in the Third General Hospital in London, where the patients included the grievously wounded and those driven insane by shell-shock. Nevinson's own fragile health collapsed with rheumatic fever; he was invalided out of the army in January 1916.

Convalescence gave him a respite in which he was able to paint. The pictures he now produced, based on his memories of the experiences of the previous months, were exhibited in London in September 1916.

C. R. W. Nevinson, *Troops Resting*
Oil, 28 × 36 ins
The normal procedure of British troops on the line of march was to march for fifty-five minutes and halt for five. One wonders if the French army, shown here, had similar habits. It was not worth the infantrymen removing the heavy packs which weighed them down during the brief halts.

C. R. W. Nevinson, *A Group of Soldiers*
Oil, 36 × 24 ins
Staunchness and good humour permeate this evocative painting. Away from the front line, weapons are carefully protected from the all-pervading mud.

C. R. W. Nevinson, *Paths of Glory*
Oil, 18 × 24 ins
This sombre picture took the artist closer to the 'sharp end' of warfare, as it were, than any other. It was painted in 1917, but does not seem to have been exhibited until after the censorship ban on any depiction of dead British soldiers had been lifted.

They made a great impression. His semi-Cubist style struck a harsh note which was in keeping with the subjects; his uncomfortable imagery exactly suited the sufferings of the wounded soldiers. It was the success of this exhibition which brought him to the attention of the Department of Information.

He went to France as a war artist in 1917. He was there for little more than four weeks, returning just after the ghastly Battle of Passchendaele had started. In this brief time Nevinson was able to store up a mass of memories, including episodes of the war in the air. He worked at fever pitch on his return, having no fewer than sixty canvases ready for exhibition six months later in March 1918.

After the war he was never able to harness his talents adequately. He had the great misfortune to paint his finest pictures of subjects which almost everybody in the 1920s wanted to do their best to forget as far as possible. Naturally he continued to work, often painting townscapes from windows in London, Paris and New York; he also etched, painted genre and flower pictures, and made lithographs. Elected an ARA in 1939, he was again a war artist in World War II, with no very striking results; his career ended sadly and suddenly with a severe stroke in 1942, and he died in 1946.

C. R. W. Nevinson, *Marching Men*
Gouache, 5½ × 8 ins
Even in 1916, or so this picture suggests, some French troops were still wearing blue coats and scarlet trousers, as they had in the Franco-Prussian War of 1870.

C. R. W. Nevinson, *The Food Queue*
Pastel, 20 × 26 ins
For the first time in British history, queuing for food became a regular part of daily life. Progressive food shortages led to the introduction of rationing early in 1917.

ERIC HENRI KENNINGTON was born in Chelsea in 1888. His mother was Swedish in origin, his father an artist, a portrait painter and the first secretary of the New English Art Club. After education at St Paul's School (then in Hammersmith) and at the Lambeth School of Art, the young Kennington also started painting portraits, first exhibiting at the Royal Academy in 1908.

On the outbreak of war he at once enlisted in the 'Kensingtons', the 13th London Regiment. He served with this unit as a private until he was invalided out of the army in June 1915. He had been in France for many months, and had been in action in the trenches. Convalescence gave him, too, the opportunity to paint. *The Kensingtons at Laventie*, exhibited in the spring of 1916, caused something of a sensation. Painted in a robust but conventional style, his down-to-earth portrayal of exhausted and unglamorous soldiers was, at the time, something new.

The success of this exhibition encouraged Kennington to seek

Eric Kennington, *The Kensingtons at Laventie*
Oil on glass, 55 × 60 ins
Although he joined the unit a few weeks after Eric Kennington had been invalided home, John F. Tucker, the author of *Johnny Get Your Gun*, was able to identify all the soldiers concerned. From the left they are Private McCafferty, Private Eric Kennington, Private W. Harvey, Private Guy, Lance-Corporal Wilson, Private Slade and Corporal J. Kealey. The exhausted figure on the ground is Private A. Todd. The polished brasses and the captured *pickelhaube* (spiked helmets) confirm the early date of this scene; but the carefully protected rifles and the 'eating irons' tucked into the puttees could have been seen at any time during the war.

employment as a war artist. He had enough support in the corridors of power for this to be agreed, and he returned to France in August 1917. Here he found his best subjects among the ordinary soldiers, for whom he had boundless admiration; his portraits were often in pastel, a medium which suited both the needs of the time and his own inclinations. Kennington was also fascinated by all the varieties of the soldiers' accommodation, the huts and tents of the rear areas, and the lean-tos and rat-ridden dug-outs of the front line. But he concentrated on 'the magnificence of the men', which, of course, he knew at first hand.

In the post-war years Kennington became best known to the general public for his striking illustrations of Arab leaders and others in T. E. Lawrence's *The Seven Pillars of Wisdom*. However, most of his energies went into sculpture, which he took up after carving a memorial to the men in the division in which he had served in 1915. He served again as a war artist in World War II, again using pastels as a medium for scores of portraits of fighting men, both notable and unknown. He became an RA in 1959, the year before he died.

In the context of artists of World War I, the name of PAUL NASH is the most important. At the time his war paintings, more than any others, made, and have continued to make, a unique and indelible impression on the public consciousness. His images of war are at once highly accessible and totally memorable. Without being unfair to either man, Nash can be said to be the artist equivalent of the poet Wilfred Owen.

Born in 1889, Paul Nash was the son of a successful lawyer, from prosperous Buckinghamshire yeoman stock; his mother's family background was that of the Royal Navy. And it was for the navy that Nash was originally intended. In those days, naval cadets went to Osborne or Dartmouth when they were twelve or thirteen. Nash failed the entrance examination, and went instead to St Paul's School. This he left when seventeen, starting his training as an artist at the Chelsea Polytechnic, moving on to the London County Council (LCC) Technical School in Bolt Court. At this point he was advised by William Rothenstein to go on to the Slade School, which he duly did in 1910.

At this time, as at others, the Slade had some very talented students. Stanley Spencer, Mark Gertler, William Roberts, Edward Wadsworth and C. R. W. Nevinson were among Nash's contemporaries. The prevailing style at the school was conventional. It was at this time that Tonks solemnly warned all the Slade students against contamination from Post-Impressionism, telling them not to visit the Post-Impressionist exhibition. This absurd advice was certain to ensure that all the students did go to this famous show, forbidden fruit always being the

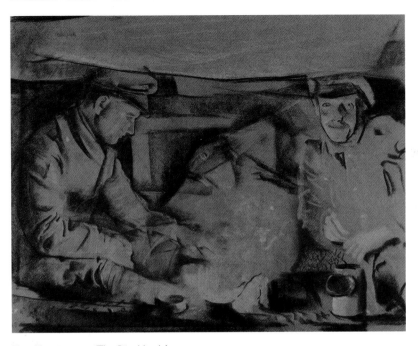

Eric Kennington, 'The Die-Hards'
Pastel, 19 × 25¼ ins
The Die-Hards, the Army's nickname for the Middlesex Regiment dating from the Battle of Albuera of 1811, are out of the line, in billets, in comparative safety and luxury.

Eric Kennington, *A Famous Raider, of the Lancashire Fusiliers*
Lithograph, 15¼ × 18½ ins
Raiding enemy trenches was a commonplace night-time activity, usually carried out with the capture of prisoners in mind, thus building up intelligence about the enemy forces in the area. It was, of course, very hazardous indeed.

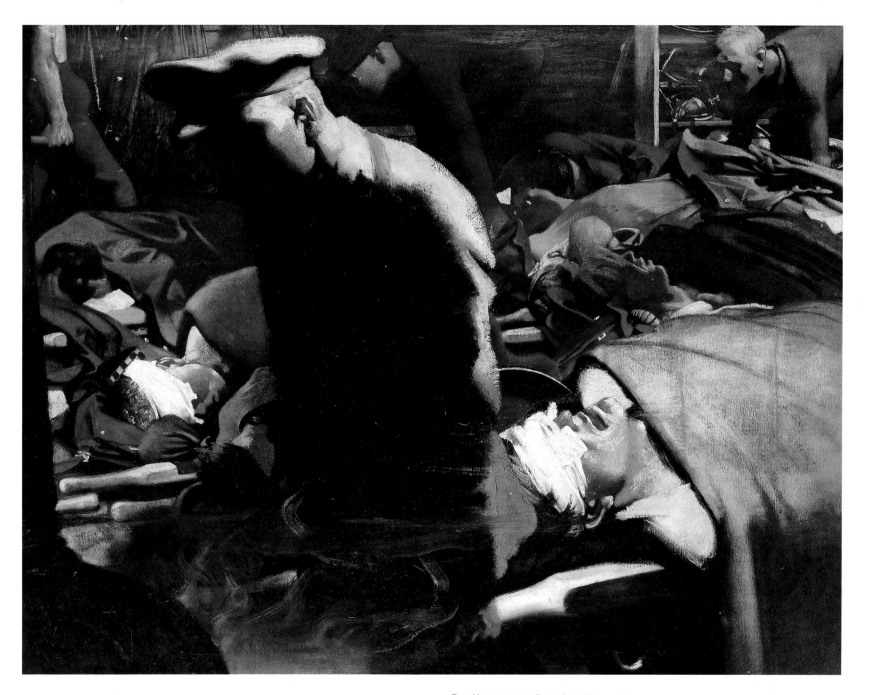

Eric Kennington, *Gassed and Wounded*
Oil, 28 × 36 ins
Poison gas was first used by the German army, on an experimental basis, on 27
October 1914 in the Neuve Chapelle district. Their first substantial gas attack was
launched at Ypres on 22 April 1915. The British first responded at Loos on 25
September 1915.

Paul Nash, *We Are Making a New World*
Oil, 28 × 36 ins
No figures are to be seen, nor any of the debris of war; yet this is a nightmare landscape, distorted and harrowed.

Paul Nash, *Spring in the Trenches, Ridge Wood, 1917*
Oil, 24 × 20 ins
Ridge Wood lies about three miles south of Ypres, near Vierstraat. The wood is not much more than a copse, and the ridge not much more than a hummock. Yet the sun shines, the birds sing and even a few leaves are doing their best to grow on the stricken trees.

Eric Kennington, *A Camouflaged Tent*
Black chalk, 7½ × 11¼ ins
The army's nineteenth-century bell tent remained in use in World War II. Activity by aircraft demanded the use of camouflage, even in the areas where tents were used for sleeping.

Eric Kennington, *The Dismantled 'Elephant' Hut*
Pastel on grey paper, 18½ × 24½ ins
Nissen huts were nicknamed Elephant huts.

most enticing – but it has to be said that few students seem to have been much influenced by their first sight of Cézanne and the other masters on display.

Paul Nash was an unusual student. All accounts mention his very noticeable neatness in attire, which alone would tend to make him unusual. He was also a voracious reader, much influenced by Tennyson, Morris, Keats, Whitman and Borrow, but most of all by the two painter-poets Rossetti and Blake. Of these, Blake and Borrow led him towards nature and landscape, intensifying his own natural inclinations. Places were always to mean much to him – the Wittenham

Clumps, for example, a well-known landmark in a wide Thames valley area which he first saw in 1909 on a visit to an uncle in the neighbourhood, were to become a potent image throughout his life. Paul Nash was also advised, somewhat unexpectedly, by the RA Sir William Richmond: 'Go in for nature, my boy.' In his pre-war work, largely conventional and in watercolour, Nash did indeed go in for nature, which he depicted carefully and industriously with trees as the main subject of his pictures. He had one-man shows in 1912 and 1913 without making much of an impression.

Enlisting in the Artists' Rifles in 1914, he was commissioned a second lieutenant in the Hampshire Regiment in 1916. His service with the Hampshires included active service in France, some of it in the trenches of the Ypres salient. It was this experience, of not many weeks' duration, which immeasurably deepened and intensified his perceptions.

Paul Nash was a methodical person and also the sort of artist who

Paul Nash, *The Menin Road*
Oil, 72 × 125 ins
Paul Nash's largest, and justly most renowned, World War I picture. Leaving Ypres (or Ieper) by the Menin Gate, the Menin Road (N9) runs south-eastwards towards Menin (or Menen) eleven miles away.

Paul Nash, *The Ypres Salient at Night*
Oil, 28 × 36 ins
In military parlance, a salient in a line of fortifications is an angle or a bulge extending into enemy territory. The salient in front of Ypres was held by the British throughout the war. Night was always a busy time in the trenches: reliefs took place; rations and supplies were brought forward; the wounded were taken back; trenches were repaired; raids were made; barbed-wire entanglements were augmented.

Paul Nash, *Existence*
Black chalk and watercolour, 19 × 12¾ is
Vaguely reminiscent of Bruce Bairnsfather's cartoon character 'Old Bill', this study
is a powerful tribute to the stoic fortitude of the front-line soldiers.

never stopped working – there have always been artists of this kind, as there have always been those who are obliged to sandwich creative spells between periods of artistic regeneration. Nash snatched every opportunity which came his way to observe and to make notes and sketches. All soldiers know, only too well, that even during active service in the front line there are often times when there is nothing whatever to do, except to remain calm and alert. Boredom is an enemy, as are bullets, but artists such as Nash are never bored, always being able to see and record, even in the most unpromising situations.

He was, of course, fortunate to survive at all in the Ypres salient, even though he spent only a short spell there. He was more fortunate still to have been invalided home in May 1917, suffering from a rib broken in an unmilitary accident. He escaped the appalling risks of the holocaust of the Passchendaele battle which started a couple of months later, and started, moreover, in the Ypres salient. Recuperating in London, the assiduous Paul Nash worked so rapidly on the sketches he had made in France that an exhibition of them was held in July 1917. This attracted a great deal of favourable attention.

Nash's poetic imagination, far from being crushed by the horrendous events of the war, expanded to meet those events and to produce images all the more terrible for being so precise, so detached and sometimes almost abstract. Their straightforward style made them accessible to all, but there was more to it than mere accessibility. These haunting interpretations of the Flanders battlefields are especially memorable because of the way in which Nash's poetic gift was able to transmute the grimly appalling scenes into works of remarkable, if macabre, beauty. He was able to reach beyond the superficial aspects of all he had seen, and fix the desolation in enduring pictures.

It is striking that it was on nature which Paul Nash mostly focused. It was the desolation of the countryside on such a huge scale which most outraged him: the tortured fields, pitted with shell holes and churned to mud, the nightmare skeletons of trees. The equal horror which he felt at the human miseries, made plain in his letters to his wife, found a most powerful expression in paintings in which human figures often play a very minor part, or none at all. Yet his human understanding is apparent, made clear in his own artistic language.

The success of Nash's exhibition led, in November 1917, to his appointment as a war artist. As he remained a second lieutenant, this was a matter of effecting a transfer to his new post. He went back to France, remaining for only a couple of months. But this well-organised and assiduous man was able to produce in this time a mass of new material from which he developed many more striking and admirable pictures when back in England. He was now often using oils, which intensified his self-expression and powers of communication.

Much of this work appeared in a further exhibition, in March 1918, an influential event which again caused a stir. He showed again how he was able to distil poetic image from the very depths of infinite horror. Often the ravaged and torn trees point to the sky almost as if they represented maimed and twisted human hands. The title of one of these pictures, *We Are Making a New World*, with its echoes of William Blake, made an ironic point which all could appreciate.

It is not in the least surprising that Paul Nash was unsettled by the war. He had seen much, his style had developed rapidly and very convincingly, and he found himself with a greater audience than he had had before the war. But he could not, of course, continue to paint the pictures which had brought him that audience. He could not paint more war pictures; and, in any case, people would not have wanted to see such pictures, let alone buy them. But Nash was a determined and ambitious man, whose development as a painter was sustained throughout his life; his gifts were never allowed to run out of control.

He returned to where he had begun, to nature and the countryside, now painting with intensified feeling. Although dogged by ill-health, particularly asthma, for the rest of his life, he enlivened this mainstream of his work with numerous other activities. There was a brief spell of teaching at the Royal College of Art; he illustrated books, designed scenery and fabrics, and made some wood-engravings. He designed posters for Shell-Mex. * He wrote sometimes, including the *Shell Guide to Dorset*, the first of Shell's county guides. This book is now a collector's item. It contains many of Nash's own very skilful photographs.

But all the time this passionate lover of the countryside was continuing to paint nature, trees often playing a large part. Beech-trees in particular had a special fascination, their sun-crossed vertical lines often inspiring him. His work started to move a little nearer to Abstraction, almost in the Ivon Hitchens manner. But this tentative development did not progress further, moving rather towards Surrealism and the creation of images based on the dictates of the subconscious mind.

Paul Nash had for years collected *objets trouvés*, the use of which was part of the Surrealist method. More importantly, his wartime pictures had often shown the night-time world of the front line (where more happened at night than during the daylight hours), and these pictures certainly had a nightmare quality. The step towards Surrealism was, for Nash, a small step.

Surrealist influences can readily be seen in some of the work which he did as a war artist in World War II, when this remarkable man again produced memorable images in superbly assured and accomplished works of art. But his subsequent development as an artist can only be a matter for conjecture, as he died, tragically young, in 1946.

* At this time many younger artists designed posters for London Transport and Shell-Mex, commissioned respectively by Frank Pick and Jack Beddington. The latter, always known as 'Beddy-old-cock', built up for Shell a magnificent collection which is still carefully preserved. One of Paul Nash's posters, 'Footballers prefer Shell', characteristically included no human figures, the image being made by the pattern of the football net. This, amongst many others, became familiar to me when I worked for Shell-Mex and BP in the late 1950s.

Paul Nash, *A Howitzer Firing*
Oil, 28 × 36 ins
The howitzer, in its emplacement, is camouflaged from attack or observation from the air. Manned by a well-drilled gun crew, it could fire every fifteen seconds.

Paul Nash, *Ruined Country*
Watercolour, 11 × 15¼ ins
A scene on an old battlefield, near La Folie Wood. La Folie is a farm on the western flank of Vimy Ridge; it was captured by Canadian forces on 9 April 1917.

Sir William Rothenstein, *Ypres Salient*
Oil, 8 × 6 ins
A scene in the Ypres Salient in 1918. After more than four years, the war had moved on from this stricken area.

The last artist to be sent to France before the Department of Information became a ministry was WILLIAM ROTHENSTEIN, appointed in December 1917. Rothenstein was already an influential figure in the world of art; like Muirhead Bone he was a perceptive and generous man, more than ready to encourage young artists.

He was a shade older than Bone, having been born in 1872, the third of six children of a Bradford wool merchant, a German-born émigré. Rothenstein was therefore forty-four when appointed. Being fiercely patriotic to Britain, he was glad to go, but apprehensive. His German name and his faint German accent had led to much unpleasantness in the Gloucestershire village where he lived in the early days of the war, when rabid spy-mania was rampant. (He had decided not to change his name to Ruthersten earlier in the war, as his two brothers had – one of them was the painter and illustrator Albert Ruthersten.) He knew that artists in France were always liable to be arrested while sketching by zealous officers, and he feared they would take him for a spy. Rothenstein was not to escape this hazard and was duly arrested on one occasion: but he was in good company, as F. E. Smith, who was then Attorney-General and a Cabinet minister, had also been arrested by the military authorities when on an official visit to the army in France. This entertaining contretemps came about through malicious and adroit tampering with the text of a telegram, the culprit never being identified.

He had left his Yorkshire home aged sixteen to enrol at the Slade School in London. As it happened, this was not one of the most sparkling periods in the history of that establishment. His teacher was Alphonse Legros, a fine academic draughtsman who had once been a pupil of Ingres. But Legros was near the end of his career, and his teaching was tired and spiritless. The following year, Rothenstein moved eagerly on to the Académie Julian in Paris, where he was to remain for four years. He had an exciting time, befriended by Whistler and forming other meaningful links with Toulouse-Lautrec, with Camille Pissarro and with Degas, another link with Ingres. While still very young he had great success in the 1890s, his freshness and energy combining with his uplifting Paris training to put his pictures in demand. Much of his work, then and later, was portrait-painting.

Rothenstein was a many-faceted personality, and his style began to alter around the turn of the century. His work became increasingly earnest and intense, while he remained fanatically assiduous; a dourness came into his work, a quality which did not find general appeal. He did more work as a writer and a critic, and as such developed a hostility to Roger Fry and Post-Impressionism. He championed the establishment of provincial museums and art centres, and he became greatly interested in the art of the Indian subcontinent.

In France Rothenstein felt, wholly characteristically, at a disadvantage as compared with younger artists, such as Paul Nash, whom he greatly admired and who had seen the fighting at first hand. He went to the Somme front in December 1917, travelling about a great deal, and seemed to find great beauty in the numerous ruined buildings which by this time were scattered across northern France in profusion. A period spent painting portraits of Indian troops must have delighted him. He was with the Fifth Army in March 1918, when the Germans launched their last, desperate onslaught of the war. In the resulting chaos Rothenstein acted as an unofficial hospital orderly. Returning to England at the end of March, his resulting pictures were exhibited in May, but without making a very striking impression.

In 1920 Rothenstein became principal of the Royal College of Art, remaining in the post until 1935. As his reputation as a writer and teacher grew, his standing as an artist declined. His work had become unfashionable. Although sixty-six when World War II broke out, he nevertheless contrived to become a war artist with the Royal Air Force, working as industriously as ever and sometimes flying in bombers when every member of the crew was more than fifty years younger than he was himself. He died shortly before the end of the war, in 1945.

John Buchan was not, in official eyes, much of a success as head of the Department of Information. In February 1918 Lloyd George made some typically adroit changes to put this right, thereby also paying a personal political debt and furthermore muzzling potential opposition. Lord Northcliffe, the first and the most powerful of the press lords, owner of both the *Daily Mail* and *The Times*, was put in charge of all propaganda to enemy countries. Propaganda directed towards the Allies and the neutral countries was put in the hands of Lord Beaverbrook, owner of the *Daily Express* since 1916, with the Department of Information being simultaneously upgraded to a ministry. Beaverbrook was known to feel that his backstage activities which had, at least in his own eyes, resulted in Lloyd George's elevation to the premiership, had been insufficiently rewarded by the peerage which had then been bestowed on him.

On the face of it things looked bad for the war artists. The Literature and Art Department was greatly reduced: books and magazines were not Beaverbrook's style, which was concentrated on news, on instant journalism and on films. The staff moved out of Wellington House to be accommodated in a cramped hotel in the Strand. The auguries were not propitious.

But, as it turned out, the Canadian Beaverbrook's appointment was beneficial. Early in the war Beaverbrook, then Sir Max Aitken and MP for Ashton-under-Lyne, had become the Canadian eyewitness at GHQ in France. In this post, which he had no doubt invented for himself, he had organised a careful collection of records concerning Canada's contribution to the war effort. A Canadian War Memorial Committee had been set up which had, amongst other things, commissioned many paintings, often from British artists, as part of this record. A memorable exhibition of some of these pictures had been held at the Royal Academy in 1917.

The choice of artists had not been conventional. Beaverbrook's advisers, notably Frank Rutter, were forward-looking, while Beaverbrook himself always had an impish anti-Establishment streak in his personality. This exhibition included, for example, two huge Vorticist works, by Wyndham Lewis and by William Roberts. It was the first occasion that anything of the kind had been seen at Burlington House (and, moreover, the authentic voice of the twentieth century was not to be heard there again for something like thirty years). The examples of Vorticism bewildered most visitors while stunning some, such as the fourteen-year-old Kenneth Clark. Many responded avidly to the work of such artists as Nevinson, Paul Nash and Edward Wadsworth.

The changes at the top also brought Arnold Bennett into an influen-

Sir William Rothenstein, *Talbot House, Ypres*
Gouache, 13 × 20 ins
There is a mystery about this charming painting. The Toc H movement started in a place called Talbot House in Poperinge, seven miles or so to the west of Ypres. Can the artist have confused the two locations?

tial position, in charge of propaganda directed towards France. Bennett, later to become a powerful writer on Beaverbrook's *Evening Standard*, had lived in Paris for ten yeas, knew something of French art, and was a discerning patron in a modest way – he owned pictures by Nevinson, Nash and Roberts, for example. Bennett was fiercely anti-Academy, usually referring to the work of RAs as 'muck'.

An important result of all these changes in organisation was a change of emphasis. Pictures were no longer considered primarily as a contribution to propaganda; they were now to be thought of chiefly as a record. A British War Memorial Committee (BWMC) was established, including Beaverbrook, Bennett and Masterman. Muirhead Bone was one of this committee's chief advisers.

Of all the artists to be considered in this study, none is more enigmatic and puzzling than AUGUSTUS JOHN. He was, by universal consent, the finest natural draughtsman ever to enter the Slade School, which he had joined at the age of sixteen in 1894. His career had developed steadily from this head start and he had become, amongst other things, a brilliant if very uneven portrait painter, marrying the swagger of van Dyck to a muted Impressionism. At his best he was certainly magnificent; some of his lesser portraits were thought vulgar in the most fastidious circles.

He was the sort of flamboyant person around whom controversy is always apt to rage. His ultra-unconventional, ultra-Bohemian, almost nomadic lifestyle, his startling appearance and fierce eyes, histrionic manner, potent drinking, large entourage and growing squad of children all fascinated people, many of them no doubt as envious as they were disapproving. By 1914 he was undoubtedly the best-known artist in Britain, matching exactly what, in the public eye, an artist should be like and look like; any actor in those days who was obliged to appear on the stage as an artist simply imitated John as far as was possible. He was a very visible person, often to be seen racketing about London*.

Yet this Welshman was a most complex personality, not in the least merely the swaggering boozer the general public mostly saw. He was better informed and far better read than the chance acquaintance might have supposed. His wild appearance belied a normally courteous approach. He was a perceptive and generous friend to many lesser artists. And he was humbly disappointed with his own achievements. His whole life as an artist was to remain a constant search for a 'grand' subject, to be tackled on an heroic scale.

In this respect, the war might have proved an ideal opportunity but, tragically, it was not to be the case. John's initial enthusiasm for drilling in the courtyard of the Royal Academy soon evaporated. Always the most restless of men, he felt stultified by being unable to slip over to France at a moment's notice, something he had been doing for years. Nothing seemed to fire his imagination. He substituted Ireland for France for a time, and thought that he had stumbled on his grand subject in Galway. Everything was unsatisfactory and disturbing.

Acquaintance with Beaverbrook led to his being commissioned as a major in the Canadian army, with a brief to paint what he liked with the Canadians. He thus became the only army officer in all the Allied forces permitted to wear a beard, apart from King George V, for whom he was occasionally mistaken – a superbly ironic circumstance, as no two men can conceivably have been more unalike, apart from their bearded appearance. John went gleefully and excitedly off to France, only to return in disgrace a couple of months later after an unbecoming brawl, and saved from court-martial by Beaverbrook's intervention. He had achieved little.

Beaverbrook now suggested an enormous work for the BWMC; it was to be a giant picture symbolising the co-operation of the two main Allies, France and Britain. John went off to France again, this time to the British sector, but again was able to achieve little. Equally John's attendance at the peace conference in 1919, to which he was summoned by the government on generous terms, did not lead to the expected group portraits; although many portraits were executed, in many cases they were of persons wholly unconnected with the conference. Augustus John's mercurial temperament could not accommodate official direction, however tactful and gentle, nor could he

summon the huge persistence necessary to complete a grand picture.

Almost the only tangible result of the period of official involvement is John's canvas *Fraternity*. It is too facile to dismiss this picture as a careful copy of a *Daily Mail* photographic postcard, which indeed it is. As with many other artists, it was the warm comradeship of the soldiers which made a deep impression on John. His strength of feeling is powerfully expressed in this group, itself highly reminiscent of the poignant lines in the soldiers' song:

> Pack up your troubles in your old kit bag,
> And smile, smile, smile.
> While you've a lucifer to light your fag,
> Smile, boys, that's the style.

JOHN SINGER SARGENT was also sent out to the Western Front at this time. He too was commissioned to paint a huge canvas, meant to symbolise the co-operation between the British and American forces. Like the other large works commissioned at this time, John's for example, this picture was intended to form part of the decoration for a Hall of Remembrance. Preliminary plans for this project, later abandoned, were to reach an advanced stage – a site on Richmond Hill was in view, and the architectural work was in the hands of Charles Holden, later best known for the many tube stations which he designed for London Transport and for their headquarters above St James's Park station in Broadway.

Sargent was a tactful choice for this dubious project. He was American, and had trained as an artist in Florence and in Paris. The first portraits he attempted in Paris misfired and he rapidly moved to London; this had been in 1886, when he was thirty. He settled in London, and here he soon established himself as a virtuoso portrait painter. He supplanted the ageing Millais as the fashionable portraitist of high society, soon gaining the reputation of being the finest in London since Lawrence. Indeed his most successful portraits are dazzlingly skilful, the acme of panache, though there were some who felt that he sometimes slipped over the borderline into flashiness. He had great social as well as professional success, and was elected an RA in 1897.

He was well over sixty when he went to France in 1918. Here he was treated as a VIP. He soon abandoned the idea of painting the picture which had originally been intended, but seemed to enjoy himself painting a handful of pictures in the rear areas of the army. One day on his travels he stumbled across a casualty clearing station which happened to be busily engaged in treating scores of men afflicted with the effects

---

* This remained the case for years. I have a vivid memory of seeing John in Charing Cross Road one afternoon in the 1950s, supported by not one but two amazingly attractive girls, both of whom must have been not less than fifty years younger than the great artist.

Augustus John, *Fraternity*
Oil, 93½ × 57 ins
The soldiers' uniforms and equipment are detailed with precision. They are not encumbered by their 'large packs'; nor are their Lee-Enfield rifles fitted with bayonets.

John Singer Sargent, *A Street in Arras*
Watercolour, 15½ × 20¾ ins
Soldiers of a Highland regiment resting outside a building damaged by shellfire.
The German army were within two miles of Arras in April 1918, but had been
pushed back by August, when Sargent painted this scene.

of mustard gas (fortunately usually temporary). He at once saw the
enormous potential of this subject. His resulting picture, *Gassed*, is one
of the most memorably haunting images of the war. An unforgettable
composition, it is grouped with all the masterful skill of the veteran
Sargent. He died in 1925.

John Singer Sargent, *Gassed*
Oil, 90 × 240 ins
The dressing station that Sargent encountered was near Le Bac-de-Sud, on the Doullens–Arras road (N25); this was in August 1918. He depicted men made temporarily blind by mustard gas arriving in parties of half-a-dozen, led by an orderly.

HENRY TONKS was also sent out to the Somme front, with Sargent. This was certainly an unusual pairing, as the two men were very different both as artists and as people – but of course they were not expected to work together.

Tonks came from a solid middle-class Birmingham family and he had the conventional schooling of the middle class, all of which he greatly detested, always afterwards referring to his public school as 'that damnable Clifton'. Tonks studied medicine, starting as an eighteen-year-old student in Brighton and moving two years later, in 1882, to the London Hospital for a further three years. During these years drawing started to absorb his energies, but he went on to qualify as an FRCS and took up a consultant post at the Royal Free Hospital.

Now he began to attend classes in drawing at the LCC's Technical Institute. It was here that he made the acquaintance of Frederick Brown, and when the latter was appointed principal of the Slade School he persuaded Tonks to abandon medicine and become an assistant teacher at the Slade. At the same time the much more conventional appointment of Wilson Steer as another assistant teacher was made.

There is no doubt that this teaching team was active at a most inspiring period in the history of the Slade. Tonks played a full part in this. In spite of his aversion to Post-Impressionism (and to all other -isms, in fact to all 'modern art'), and in spite of his notorious

Henry Tonks, *An Underground Casualty Clearing Station, Arras*
Oil, 22 × 28 ins
There were obvious advantages in being able to treat wounds in comparative safety such as that offered by a large cellar. One of the purposes of a casualty clearing station was to sort out the destination for each wounded man and arrange for his onward transportation, perhaps by motor ambulance.

Henry Tonks, *An Advanced Dressing Station in France, 1918*
Oil, 72 × 86 ins
Casualties of all sorts, including a file of men blinded by mustard gas, are arriving
in a steady stream of walking wounded. Advanced dressing stations were not
equipped to deal with serious cases, which were moved back at the first
opportunity.

misjudgements (such as those concerning Matthew Smith and Nevinson), he proved to be an effective teacher. He was that rare phenomenon, an authentic academic artist, combining skills which are a positive attribute in any teacher of drawing since skill in draughtsmanship was and remains a basic requirement for any artist. Tonks had a strange, quirky personality, at once warm and chilly; he could be suspicious, secretive, touchy, and jealous, and was not without a streak of malignity. He was to be less successful when he came to preside over the Slade School as principal, a post he held from 1917 to 1930. He died, unmarried, in 1937.

Tonks returned to medicine on the outbreak of war, working at first in a civilian capacity before joining the Royal Army Medical Corps in 1916. Here he became involved in plastic surgery, then in its infancy, but a discipline in which his skills as both an artist and a surgeon could be deployed effectively. When in 1918 he was gathered into the world of the war artists, he was already both a commissioned officer of non-combatant status, and the principal of the country's premier art school, to which post he had been appointed in absentia. Neither of these attributes really qualified him for work as a war artist; he was also a man with a horror of criticism, which made working in public a torture for him. These feelings perhaps emanated from his curious, semi-amateur

start in the art world, so very different from the prolonged apprenticeship of such artists as Sargent.

Tonks' work in France was not altogether effective. His monumental *An Advanced Dressing Station in France* has been criticised as being a series of un-coordinated life studies rather than a coherent whole, with little in the way of links between one part of the canvas and another; but another view of this picture is that it is 'a monumental work in the authentic academic tradition'.

Tonks also seems to have been the only war artist to have found his way to the north Russian front, part of the British contribution to the anti-Bolshevik war fought in 1919.

CHARLES SIMS was another senior figure from the art world who was sent out to the Western Front in late 1918; he went out to Arras in October, again with a large canvas in view. A quiet and thoughtful man, Sims was born in Islington in 1873, the son of a costume-manufacturer; he had a prolonged artistic education, studying successively at the Royal College of Art, the Académie Julian in Paris and at the Royal Academy Schools. He painted genre and landscape with great skill. He also painted mystical and fantastic themes and became well known in Edwardian days as a portrait painter. He was to be underrated for many years, although dutifully represented in the Tate Gallery. His work as a war artist was almost limited to the large canvas he had been sent out to paint.

An RA from 1915, Sims was to become Keeper of the Royal Academy in 1920. But this led to triumph and tragedy. In 1924 he was commissioned to paint an official portrait of King George V. He turned out a brilliant portrait but he had, most lamentably, become fascinated by the King's elegant legs, which were given a shade of undue prominence. The monarch complained that he had been made to look like a ballet dancer; he detested the portrait and, in a moment of irascibility for which he was famous, ordered the destruction of the picture. In due course the portrait was burnt, and burnt moreover at the Royal Academy. Sims naturally reacted to this scurvy treatment; deeply disillusioned, he resigned his Academy post. Not long after this, in 1928, he was to take his own life.

Early in November 1918 Sims was joined by another artist, in this case one of those plucked from active service. This was the little-known COLIN GILL (not related to the far more widely known sculptor and designer Eric Gill). Colin Unwin Gill was best known as a painter of historical, and other, mural decorations, but he also painted genre works and portraits. Born in Kent in 1892, he had trained at the Slade School and had started exhibiting, at the New English Art Club, in 1914.

Gill enlisted in the Royal Artillery in 1914 and served in France from 1915, being seconded to the Royal Engineers the following year as a camouflage officer. His work as an official war artist was all done after the Armistice of 11 November 1918; it is unexcitingly competent, and it has to be said that he was a surprising choice for one of the pictures intended for the Hall of Remembrance.

His post-war work was concentrated on decorative murals. He was working on a project of this kind in Johannesburg when he died suddenly, in 1940.

Another artistic heavyweight to be sent to France, in this case in November 1918, was D. Y. CAMERON, later to become Sir David. He was a successful landscape painter and etcher of the Glasgow School. The son of a minister of the Scottish church in Glasgow, Cameron fell in love with art while still at school at Glasgow Academy.

He started work in an ironfounder's offices, hating it unreservedly and spending as much time as he could at night classes at the Glasgow School of Art. Eventually, in 1885, aged twenty, he was released from his daily torment when he went to the Mound School of Art in Edinburgh. His career as an artist developed rapidly; he travelled widely on the Continent; he had great energy, enthusiasm and persistence and, by 1918, much experience.

After some work for the Canadians he painted a large canvas for the BWMC, *The Battlefield of Ypres*, a masterful composition based on the many sketches which he had made in France. 'It is not a portrait of any one spot,' he said. 'Photographers can do that.' But it has a bleak message which distils all Cameron's feelings with most powerful effect.

Charles Sims, *A Camouflaged Quarry*
Oil, 17 × 29 ins
This very large quarry was near Cherisy, about six miles south-east of Arras. It contained many caves cut into the chalk, which had been carefully camouflaged by the Germans and used as dug-out shelters; they were lit by electricity.

Colin Gill, *Evening, after a Push*
Oil, 30 × 20 ins
'Push' was a slang euphemism for attack. Here, it seems that dispirited troops are taking advantage of the semi-darkness to move back, under a sky lit by searchlights and enlivened by captive observation balloons.

Sir David Cameron, *The Battlefield of Ypres*
Oil, 72 × 125 ins
This very large picture, one of those intended for the Hall of Remembrance, does not depict any particular spot in the Ypres area. It is a composite image, made all the more memorable by its sense of stillness and its haunting emptiness.

John Nash, *Over the Top*
Oil, 31¼ × 42¼ ins
The unit is the 1st Artists' Rifles; the date, 30 December 1917; the place, Marcoing. Five miles south-east of Cambrai, Marcoing had been taken by the British in November and recaptured by the Germans a week later. The Artists' Rifles action is described on pages 64–5.

JOHN NASH, by four years the younger brother of Paul, was born in 1893 and was another war artist who was appointed after active service. He saw much of this in his time and his experiences gave him the material for some very powerful pictures; some people believe that his work is the greatest of all the World War I war artists.

He was brought up in Buckinghamshire from 1901, when his family moved there. The landscape of the Chilterns was to be a perpetual

John Nash, *Stand-to before Dawn*
Pen and watercolour, 13 × 15½ ins
The hour before dawn, always the most likely hour for an enemy attack,
demanded total vigilance in the trenches. All is prepared, in this study of nervous
readiness.

John Nash, *Oppy Wood, Evening, 1917*
Oil, 72 × 84 ins
Oppy is a village in the Vimy district. It had been fortified by the Germans, and
was one of the strongest positions on the whole Western Front. The village, and
the wood, were both eventually captured in September 1918, after heavy fighting.

influence on him. He was at school at Wellington College and was vir-
tually self-taught as an artist, having been advised by his brother to
avoid all art schools. His work was first shown in 1913, in an exhibition
which he and Paul organised independently. Through his brother, too,
he got to know, and received much encouragement from, such artists as
Sickert, Rothenstein and Robert Bevan. Perhaps partly because he had
never been a student with other art students, he was to become a somewhat isolated figure, not classified, joined or linked with other artists in
real or supposed groupings. He seemed to stand to one side and go his
own way.

Enlisting in the 1st Artists' Rifles in September 1916, he saw active
service from November 1916 until January 1918. That spring he
became an official war artist. Seemingly not having made sketches in
the trenches, unlike his brother, he worked entirely from memory and
to great effect, his matter-of-fact pictures having total authenticity and
much latent power.

His greatly admired *Over the Top*, which includes a self-portrait, is
unusual in that it records an actual event which occurred in the early
morning of 30 December 1917, at a position known as Welsh Ridge
not far from Cambrai. The 1st Artists' Rifles had been withdrawn to the

John Nash, *An Advanced Post, Day*
Oil, 30 × 40 ins
By 1917, the British army no longer manned the front-line trenches continuously
with a thin line of troops. Instead, isolated strong-points were held, with larger
numbers of men in reserve trenches. Rarely did much happen during daytime;
while sentries kept watch, the men slept, the nights being too full of activity for
sleep.

relative safety of the support line, when it was called back to the front line to make an ill-considered and almost wholly disastrous counter-attack in freezing weather. *Over the Top* marks the first moment of this counter-attack. The company in which Sergeant John Nash commanded the bombing section, already reduced to eighty men, now suffered a further sixty-eight casualties, killed or wounded, in a matter of minutes. Nash was one of the fortunate dozen in the company to survive unscathed. It is not surprising that the artist was to retain in his mind's eye all the details of this grisly moment, the terrifying instant when soldiers had to struggle out of the trenches to advance across the open ground of no-man's-land.

His name made almost entirely by his war pictures, John Nash returned as soon as possible to the landscape painting which absorbed him. He painted the countryside, especially that of Buckinghamshire and of Suffolk, with quiet and lyrical passion. He was a noted illustrator, and a teacher at the Ruskin School in Oxford and later at the Royal College of Art. He was also a flower-painter, a keen fisherman and a notable gardener. Extraordinarily detached, he was said to read little apart from seed catalogues; and he seemed contented, free from ambition. Most of all he was a countryman, lovingly painting landscape with a countryman's eye. His style reached maturity astonishingly early for one who was self-taught; and his methods did not alter over the years, his vision seemingly unaffected by the powerful images which he conjured from his own experiences of World War I.

John Nash was to serve as a war artist in World War II, before transferring to a more active role in the Royal Marines. An RA from 1951, he died in 1977, still painting in Constable country, which he felt as strongly about as had Constable himself.

John Nash, *A Bombing Post in the Snow*
Pen, black chalk and watercolour, 10¼ × 18 ins
The artist was a bombing or grenade-throwing specialist, and was wholly familiar with such isolated outposts as this.

War artists, like any other grouping of artists, were a very mixed bunch, with an enormous range of personality represented amonst them; but of them all, the strangest was surely PERCY WYNDHAM LEWIS. He was a quarrelsome and suspicious character, well beyond the borders of paranoia, and he was also a creator of mysteries about himself. In later life he was perversely enigmatic, even about the date and place of his birth.

In fact this event took place in 1882 off the coast of Nova Scotia, where his American parents happened to be in their yacht. His early days are shrouded in mystery, but he was certainly at Rugby School in 1897 and 1898 (although apparently nobody ever claimed in later years to have known him at the school). Equally certainly he was at the Slade School from 1898 to 1901. Whatever may have occurred at Rugby, he did not fail to get at cross-purposes with Tonks while at the Slade; although other examples have shown that this was by no means difficult to achieve. After his time at the Slade, Lewis travelled widely on the Continent, although based mainly in Paris. He returned to England in 1909. His brilliant draughtsmanship, which had rivalled that of Augustus John in his student days, was now allied to a wide and formidable international artistic education. Although ostensibly wholly uninterested in the past, he paradoxically thought of himself as a classical artist.

He also came to rationalise his quarrelsome nature by extolling the great benefits of isolation, both for an artist and for a critic. He was already a writer and propagandist of great strength. Many artists throughout history have also been writers of quality – Reynolds' *Discourses*, Haydon's *Autobiography*, the poems of Blake and of Rossetti, Augustus John's memoirs *Chiaroscuro*, are all examples of the pen being as mighty as the brush. Wyndham Lewis not only wrote many essays and much powerful criticism, but he was also almost unique in becoming a novelist of well-regarded quality; Mervyn Peake is the only other artist-novelist who comes readily to mind. Lewis' first novel, *Tarr*, written in 1914, was published in 1918. Like most first novels, it is highly autobiographical in content.

As an artist, Lewis was quick to realise that the most significant grouping of artists in Britain at the time was the Camden Town School. He became a founder-member in 1911, although at the time his own style was strongly Cubist in character and very different from the work of Sickert, Gilman and Gore, the stalwarts of the group. Lewis soon moved on to invent Vorticism. In one sense this was his own brand of Cubism; in another, it was a reaction to Futurism; most of all, perhaps, it embodied Lewis himself, anti-everything else.

Vorticism attacked the sentimentality of nineteenth-century art; it celebrated violence, energy and the machine, while paradoxically attacking the Futurist obsession with speed. The Vorticist movement (the first British movement in art since the Pre-Raphaelites) culminated

Wyndham Lewis, *A Battery Shelled*
Oil, 72 × 125 ins
As well as the standard 18-pounder field gun, the British Army employed 4.5-inch howitzers, 60-pounder field guns, 9.2-inch howitzers and 12-inch howitzers which operated from railways. Counter-battery fire, as depicted by Lewis, was standard artillery practice.

in a London exhibition in 1915. It had its own short-lived magazine, edited and very largely written by Lewis and by Ezra Pound, called *Blast!*. This was first published in June 1914 and became famous afterwards for its long lists of the blasted and the blessed. The revolutionary excitement of Vorticism was usually expressed visually, in abstract terms, with bold lines, sharp angles and tilted planes. Lewis' chief disciples in the Vorticist movement were Frederick Etchells, William Roberts, C. R. W. Nevinson and Edward Wadsworth.

Some of these, with Lewis, were to be involved in Roger Fry's Omega Workshops in 1913. This association ended, inevitably and violently, in a blazing row in which, for once, Lewis seemed to have ample justification. It was to lead to life-long enmity between Lewis and 'Bloomsbury', whose adherents he was to attack henceforward on every opportune and inopportune occasion. In reaction he started the Rebel Art Centre, another short-lived venture.

In March 1916 Wyndham Lewis felt that his career, both as an artist and as a writer, was about to expand with explosive success. Yet he chose this moment to enlist as a gunner in the Royal Artillery. By May 1917 he was serving with a battery on the Western Front and by chance he encountered Orpen, who treated the younger artist with characteristic generosity. Although Lewis despised both Orpen and his work, he was at once consumed with jealousy, deeply envious of the extraordi-

Wyndham Lewis, *Walking Wounded*
Ink, watercolour and gouache, 10 × 15 ins
Walking wounded were able, if the trenches were adequate, to take themselves back to the Regimental Aid Post to have their wounds dressed during the day. The more severely wounded, who would be carried on a stretcher by four men, often had to wait for darkness, as it was too difficult to get the load through the trenches and the journey had to be made above ground.

nary life-style which Orpen had contrived for himself (see page 27). It made his mouth water, he said, and he at once set about extricating himself from his role in his battery. This he was able to achieve through his friendship with P. G. Konody, the art critic of *The Observer*, who was one of Beaverbrook's advisers.

The Canadian authorities duly complied, sending Lewis as a war artist to the Vimy Ridge sector of the front early in 1918. One of the pictures to result from this period was Lewis' *A Battery Shelled*, which was to be one of the most controversial paintings of the whole war (William Roberts' *A Shell Dump* was another picture in this category). Augustus John, who was also with the Canadians at this time, had known Lewis first in his Paris days and retained a wary friendship with him. John commented that *A Battery Shelled* represented an attempt by Lewis to 'reduce his "Vorticism" to the level of Canadian intelligibility'.

Lewis went on to work as a war artist for the British, and produced further admirable pictures; but it has to be said that he never quite managed totally to harness the violence inherent in Vorticism into his pictures of the war. In fact, of course, the overpowering violence of the war itself blotted out the violence of Vorticism, which did not, as a movement, survive the war.

Wyndham Lewis' career continued its noisy path after the war. With hedgehog-like prickly truculence he alienated one person after another, while painting some wonderfully brilliant portraits of great insight and power. He really seemed to enjoy controversy. He became more and more secretive, not revealing his marriage to anybody for years; he lived furtively at secret addresses, using the Pall Mall Safe Deposit as an accommodation address. His most sensational effort at alienation of his friends and contemporaries came in the 1930s when he praised Hitler and espoused the British Fascists, supporting them with his usual violent enthusiasm. However, even this absurd behaviour did not prevent Augustus John from resigning in protest from the Royal Academy in 1938, when Lewis' portrait of T. S. Eliot for the Summer Exhibition was rejected.

Leaving England on the day before World War II broke out, Lewis spent the next six years in Canada and the USA, countries which he loathed in equal measure. Times were hard and his health was poor. He returned to England again at the end of the war.

He had many enemies, but even the worst of these could not have relished his next misfortune: his sight began to fail, and by the mid-1950s he was totally blind. He had, however, a staunch supporter in Sir John Rothenstein, son of Sir William (see page 52) and the director of the Tate Gallery, where a large exhibition of Lewis' work was organised. Another supporter was the artist and writer Michael Ayrton. Yet another was his publisher, Alan White of Methuen.* Lewis, a brilliant, flawed man, died in 1957.

* Working for Methuen at that time, I believe that I once had in my hands Wyndam Lewis' last work of art. This was a bookjacket design for a new edition of *Tarr* which White published in the early 1950s. I never met Lewis, but recall seeing him once getting out of a taxi in Essex Street, a strange muffled figure in dark glasses and slouch hat.

WILLIAM ROBERTS was one of the most individual of artists. His own especial style actually evolved during his time as a war artist, when his quirky, semi-mechanical, semi-tubular figures were seen for the first time. Roberts was a Cockney, the son of a carpenter, born in 1895. He left school at fourteen to embark on a seven-year apprenticeship at the printing and poster-designing firm of Causton's, in very much the same way as Alfred J. Munnings had similarly started work at Fletcher's in Norwich.

Roberts' craftsman father encouraged his son's ambitions, making him both a drawing board and an easel. Attendance at evening art classes led to Roberts winning an LCC scholarship to the Slade School, which he attended from 1910 to 1913. He started to paint in a semi-Cubist style, was briefly involved in Roger Fry's Omega Workshops, and then joined Wyndham Lewis and Frederick Etchells in the Vorticist group.

In 1916 Roberts enlisted in the Royal Artillery as a gunner, seeing active service in France. Hearing that Wyndham Lewis was working for the Canadians as a war artist, Roberts applied for a similar post. This was granted, with the proviso that 'Cubist work would be inadmissible'. He worked as a war artist simultaneously for the Canadians and the British, the latter imposing no such proviso.

William Roberts, *A Group of British Generals*
Pen and watercolour, 5¼ × 4 ins
Never a respecter of persons, the artist plainly saw something comical about this group of General Staff officers.

William Roberts, *Burying the Dead after a Battle*
Black crayon, 20 × 17 ins
The burial party's mournful task is viewed with a sardonic eye; the precision of the foreground figures contrasts sharply with the stylised and active background.

William Roberts, *A Shell Dump, France*
Oil, 72 × 125 ins
The largest of Roberts' contributions to the collection of the Imperial War
Museum, this elaborate composition is an excellent example of the artist's highly
individual vision.

Vorticism had the effect of releasing Roberts' work from rigidly
Cubist techniques and pointing him in the direction he wished to go.
His own peculiar idiom adapted Cubism and Vorticism to his individ-
ual needs, his style not altogether unreminiscent of Fernand Léger.
This style was not only very well suited to his war pictures but was to last
him, so to speak, for the rest of his working life.

His subjects after the war were based firmly on his Cockney background. Whatever activity his strange figures, with their curious leaden
gestures, are engaged in (cycling, picnicking, talking), they are
observed with precision, wit and sardonic humour. They are, moreover, always assembled in an overall pattern of classical form. Roberts

was a master of composition, his arrangements balanced and elegant.

A short, rosy-cheeked figure of a man, William Roberts had a certain
grim persistence. He was a tough, taciturn, rigid and totally un-
intellectual figure; but he knew what he wanted to do, and went
steadily ahead doing it, not without financial difficulties in his early
days – the completion of his contract as a war artist, for example,
brought instant problems. He taught at the Central School of Art for
no less than thirty-five years. He emerged suddenly and briefly in the
1950s as a brilliant and completely unexpected master of the written
word – stung into issuing pamphlets by extravagant and, he thought,

William Roberts, *'Feeds Round': Stable-time in the Wagon-lines, France*
Oil, 20 × 24 ins
Care of the horses was of vital concern in mounted and transport units. Here the
NCOs at the right are clearly insistent that the various tasks are being carried out
correctly.

William Roberts. 18

Rosières Valley 1918.

Signallers Laying a Wire

Wyndham Lewis. In this episode he was thought to have defeated the far more experienced Lewis, a formidable achievement in itself. An ARA from 1958, Roberts became an RA in 1966; he died, at eighty-five, in 1980.

HENRY LAMB was another doctor-artist. Like Henry Tonks, he was a refugee in the world of art from the world of medicine. He was born in 1883, not long before his father was appointed Professor of Mathematics at Manchester University, and his background was academic – though he later described his time as a schoolboy at Manchester Grammar School as 'eight years of misery'. From there he went on to Manchester University as a medical student. When almost qualified as a doctor, his spare-time passion for drawing unexpectedly won him a prize in an art competition. This was all the encouragement he needed. He at once threw up his medical training and became an art student more or less overnight. He was one of those who studied at the Orpen–John school in Chelsea, and he also trained in Paris.

He was greatly influenced by John, and was swept into the Augustus John entourage for a while. In Margaret Kennedy's best-selling novel of the 1920s, *The Constant Nymph*, the bohemian patriarch surrounded by a complex retinue of wives, children, mistresses and hangers-on is said to be a caricature of John, though pictured as a musician rather than an artist. In this book the anti-hero, Lewis Dodd, is supposedly modelled on Henry Lamb, though he too is portrayed as a musician.

Regarded as devastatingly handsome in his youth, Lamb was also, for a time, the object of Lytton Strachey's passion, which was not returned but was only terminated by Lamb's first marriage. This association led to Lamb's portraits of Strachey, the most famous of which, now in the Tate Gallery, made Lamb's reputation when it was first exhibited. The Bloomsbury Group were, amongst other things, a mutual admiration society highly skilled in promoting one another's talents. Lamb benefited from this in the immediate pre-war years.

On the outbreak of war Lamb, in a highly un-Bloomsbury fashion, hastened to complete his medical training. As soon as he was qualified as a doctor he joined the Royal Army Medical Corps, serving for the rest of the war as a regimental medical officer. Like so many other army doctors he was decorated for gallantry, winning the Military Cross. He saw service in Salonika, in Palestine and on the Western Front, where he was badly gassed not long before the Armistice in November 1918.

His paintings of the war, concentrated on the Palestine campaign, were produced in the immediate post-war period. Lamb then returned placidly to his pre-war career, painting landscape and portraits, and being especially noted for his portraits of children. With his associations with Augustus John and Lytton Strachey, Henry Lamb's career and personality are especially well documented. He figures in many books of biography and autobiography, including the memoirs of Anthony Powell, who was to marry the younger sister of Lamb's second wife.

Although Lady Ottoline Morell had been an early patron and in spite of his association with Lytton Strachey, Lamb was never an integral part, a fully-paid-up member, of the Bloomsbury Group. And, while he learnt much from Augustus John, he developed his own method and his own artistic tone of voice, nowhere better exemplified than in his *Irish Troops in the Judaean Hills Surprised by a Turkish Bombardment*.

Not far off sixty when World War II began, this energetic and very attractive man served again, as an official war artist. He died in 1960.

STANLEY SPENCER was one of the war artists – perhaps the only one – who was touched with genius. Every painting by Stanley Spencer is positively and emphatically Spencerian. He devised his own idiom and invented his own artistic language, unique and unmistakable. The war years were important in his development as an artist, although they also shattered the mind of this prodigiously talented, strange, deeply religious man, who combined an almost naïve humility with great resolution. The most English of English painters, his thoughts normally never strayed far from his birthplace of Cookham on the Berkshire bank of the Thames. Of all the artists in this book, he is the only one to have a gallery dedicated to his memory in his home country*: the Stanley Spencer Gallery is in Cookham, a few yards from the house in which he was born and brought up.

He was born in modest circumstances in 1891. His patriarchal father's Bible readings to his assembled family made a life-long impression on the young Stanley, who always saw all the events of the Bible taking place in and around Cookham. After a time at the nearby Maidenhead Technical College, Stanley Spencer went to the Slade School, his tuition fees generously paid by a kindly neighbour; but after two years, in 1910, he won a scholarship, which relieved this early patron of the need to underwrite his career as a student. His very great skills as a draughtsman were soon in clear evidence, and he was highly regarded at the Slade. He himself came to look back on his student days and the work he did then as belonging to an especially golden age,

* But see Brangwyn, page 110.

William Roberts, *Rosières Valley, 1918*
Pen and watercolour, 6¼ × 10 ins
Eighteen miles south-east of Amiens, Rosières fell to the Germans in their massive attack of March 1918. This sketch of signallers laying a wire line must have been made after September of that year, when Rosières was again in British hands.

William Roberts, *During a Battle*
Pen, pencil and watercolour, 6 × 10 ins
Many telling details appear in this rapidly made and beautifully composed sketch. In the last weeks of the war on the Western Front, movement recommenced; the country now being fought over was not shattered, as can be seen here from the intact line of poplars visible on the horizon.

Henry Lamb, *Irish Troops in the Judaean Hills Surprised by a Turkish Bombardment*
Oil, 72 × 86 ins
Bivouacs and bell tents are to be seen along the rocky terraces. Men of the 10th (Irish) Division, surprised by shell-fire, hastily take cover against the terrace walls.

Sir Stanley Spencer, *Travoys Arriving with Wounded at a Dressing Station at Smol, Macedonia, September 1916*
Oil, 72 × 86 ins
The artist found an unusual and striking viewpoint for this compelling study. As in Italy in World War II, mules were found to be invaluable in the rugged Macedonian terrain. Travoys were primitive sledges, invented by North American Indians.

centred around Cookham, which he always thought of as a suburb of Heaven.

Enlisting in the Royal Army Medical Corps in 1915, he served as a private for two and a half years in Macedonia. A clumsy and (so he said) incompetent soldier, he had few opportunities to draw and, in any case, he mislaid his sketchbook in a military bath-house. He was transferred to the Royal Berkshire Regiment for a most bizarre reason which was presumably not revealed to the military authorities at the time – he had learnt that a battalion of the Berkshires was encamped at a place in the hills which he had marched through, and which had thereafter exercised an extraordinary haunting power over him. He felt compelled to return to the place, and this was a chance to do so. He went there with relief, finding some sort of peace of mind.

The powers in London had made many attempts to extricate Stanley Spencer from this humble service and commission him as a war artist – Muirhead Bone had been an early patron of the young man, and Tonks was well disposed to his former star pupil, and both urged the case. But all efforts were unsuccessful until December 1918, when the artist was invalided home with malaria. This gave the Imperial War Museum a chance, which it grabbed. Spencer's *Travoys Arriving with Wounded* was the result, painted from his powerful artistic memory and conveying effectively the peace of the military hospital after the horrors of the front line.

But Stanley Spencer's greatest war pictures were to come later. He worked and travelled but he was unsettled, his peace of mind disturbed, with his pre-war work a seemingly irrevocable dream. He even returned to the Slade for a year.

It was not until 1927 that he was able to pour out his memories of the war years. This was when he began the decorative canvases which cover the walls of the private chapel at Burghclere, a building cared for today by the National Trust. This monumental task occupied him for four years. Stanley Spencer's Burghclere paintings record, in immense and almost Pre-Raphaelite detail, all the everyday routine of the soldier's life – 'ablutions', bedmaking, breadmaking, scrubbing floors in hospital, polishing boots – everything, in fact, except fighting, which had no appeal at all for this sensitive artist. All the unlovely details are carefully set down with utmost precision and good humour, all with a well-remembered Macedonian background, and set especially in the valley which had meant so much to him at the time.

This astonishing group of paintings covers three walls of the chapel. The centrepiece is the end wall; this is devoted to the Resurrection, a theme which was to recur in Spencer's vision, often seen as occurring in Cookham churchyard. Here the dead soldiers are seen emerging from their graves in the harsh Macedonian landscape, smartening themselves up for parade, renewing friendships with their fellow-soldiers, or with their favourite mules or horses. In the background they can be seen 'handing in' the white crosses which had marked their temporary graves, and are now no longer needed. Christ is seen receiving these crosses, a sort of celestial quartermaster.

Burghclere is a compelling place, touching and unforgettable. It is so powerful in its impact that it seems as though Spencer had needed the long interval before he began this great work to recharge his spiritual batteries before he could pour out all he felt about the war.

The authorities did well to commission his official work, for in those days he was an easily derided artist whose figures could seem strange. He was always prolific and went on to be highly respected as an artist, widely represented in galleries all over the country, elected an RA in 1950, and knighted shortly before he died in 1959 – but this had by no means always been the case. He was always a bit of an odd man out; he belonged to no group or coterie; he had no followers; and he had very odd views indeed about many topics (the nature of marriage, for example). His pictures were rejected by the traditionalist Hanging Committee of the Royal Academy as late as 1935, causing him to resign as an ARA, which he had become three years earlier. Later he was harried and persecuted by one particular president of the Royal Academy, who believed that some of his work was pornographic.

He was a very small man indeed, like an animated robin, with a reddish face, pebble glasses and an urchin-like fringe of hair.* Very scruffy in appearance, he seemed even more tramp-like when he endearingly chose to push his painting gear around Cookham in an ancient pram (happily preserved in the gallery). Sublimely single-minded, happily eccentric, he was a great artist.

The Ministry of Information was not able to achieve a great deal in the minor campaigns away from the Western Front. It commissioned only one picture for the Egyptian Expeditionary Force. This was by GILBERT SPENCER, and was painted after the war had ended.

Gilbert Spencer, born in 1892, was a year younger than his brilliant brother Stanley. Growing up at Cookham, he had a lengthy artistic apprenticeship at Camberwell School of Art, at the Royal College of Art, and at the Slade School, where he studied from 1913 to 1915 and

---

* I encountered him once on a summer evening in the mid-1950s, when we went to an exhibition of his work in the church and parsonage at Cookham. The pictures were entrancing: a mixed bag, including a huge and unfinished canvas involving Christ and Cookham, a number of his poignant small square paintings recording each of the forty days Christ spent in the wilderness, and others such as some beguiling drawings of children. The artist himself was no less entrancing, chattering away unaffectedly and volubly about the great virtues of hardboard as a surface to paint on, something he had, it seemed, just discovered. 'I really can put in every blade of grass,' he said with boyish enthusiasm.

Sir Stanley Spencer, *Resurrection*
(© National Trust Photographic Library 1991/Roy Fox)
A whole wall of the Sandham Memorial Chapel at Burghclere is taken up by Spencer's *Resurrection*, a theme which constantly preoccupied the artist. Here it is taking place in the Macedonian landscape. Soldiers are emerging from their graves, smartening themselves up, being reunited with their friends and their animals, and 'handing in' the white crosses which had marked their temporary graves but are no longer required.

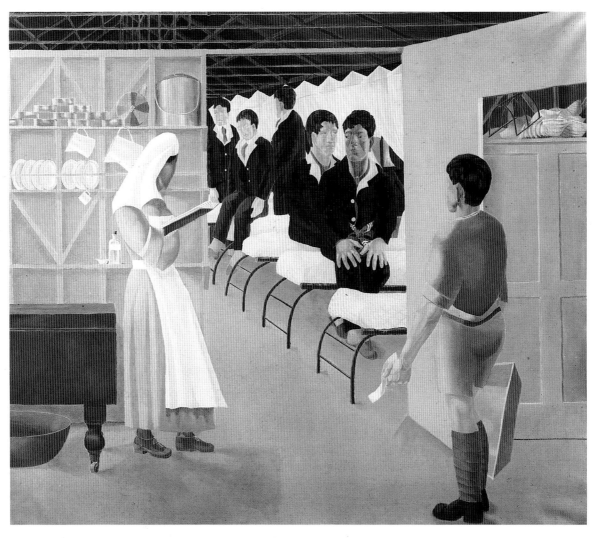

Gilbert Spencer, *New Arrivals*
Oil, 72 × 86 ins
A ward in a hospital at Mahendia, in Sinai. The latest arrivals sit on their beds, waiting for the medical officer; the sister in charge of the ward holds the records book.

again from 1919 to 1920. War was thus an interruption to his studies; apart from his war service, he never worked abroad at all, either as a student or as a working artist.

He enlisted in 1915 in the Royal Army Medical Corps, like his brother; but he too later transferred to an infantry battalion, in his case the 2/22nd London Regiment. His commissioned picture was worked from sketches he had been able to make in 1917, when he was a hospital orderly in Sinai. Spencer was still a young man when this work was painted – still a student, in fact – and his mature style had yet to

be developed. Nevertheless the picture is a fine effort, although its nature is foreign to his best work. For he became best known as a landscape painter of rare skill. His brother always maintained that Gilbert was the better landscape painter of the two; this was a generous judgement, with which not all would agree – for Stanley painted landscape beautifully, although he was not much interested in or involved with the whole process. Gilbert produced some fine portraits, both paintings and drawings, but it was landscape which absorbed him.

Never wholly overshadowed by his brother nor reacting against his voluble influence, he went his own quiet way, with admirable purpose and integrity. He became a teacher of note: at the Royal College, at Glasgow School of Art and, eventually, back where he had started himself, at Camberwell School of Art. He was a lively writer, served as an official war artist in World War II, and became an RA in 1960. He died in 1979.

Patently, the official war artists of World War I were a very mixed bunch, ranging all the way from well-established grandees such as Lavery or Orpen, well known to the public at large, right through every grade of experience to those, like Gilbert Spencer, whose employment as war artists was an interruption to their art studies and whose abilities were known to only a handful of fellow-students and teachers. Of them all, none stood higher in the esteem of artists and critics than PHILIP WILSON STEER.

Steer was born in Birkenhead in 1860, the same year as Walter

Philip Wilson Steer, *Dover Harbour, 1918*
Oil, 42 × 60 ins
Steer's major contribution shows a great deal of naval activity going on in the shadow of the famous castle and the familiar white cliffs.

Philip Wilson Steer, *Mine-Sweepers at Dover, Morning*
Watercolour, 9½ × 13½ ins
This brilliantly simple sketch has an astonishing beauty. The Dover minesweepers were busy throughout the war, helping to ensure a safe passage for the millions who made the cross-Channel journey during the conflict.

Sickert, another artist who was regarded at least as highly as Steer at that time, but who never took any official part in war art. Steer was the son of an artist and was brought up in reasonably comfortable circumstances. He went to Hereford Cathedral School, his family having moved to the Hereford district soon after his birth. The young Steer enjoyed collecting coins and at first thought of a career in the numismatic department of the British Museum; but this involved passing a Civil Service examination, and we should be grateful that this proved to be beyond his powers.

Instead he switched to art, training at first at the Gloucester School of Art and moving to the Académie Julian in Paris in 1882. Even though he never learnt to speak a word of French, Paris was to be a liberating experience for him; Whistler and Manet were the greatest influences on him. He returned to England in 1885, at once settling in Chelsea, where he was to live for the rest of his life.*

A founder-member of the New English Art Club, Steer made rapid progress. His reputation was made in the 1890s by a number of seaside pictures, many of them painted on the Suffolk coast. These were Impressionist in manner, bursting with exuberant colour and verve. Also at this time he began to teach at the Slade School, being a life-long friend of Frederick Brown, whom he had known in Paris. He remained on the staff of the Slade until Tonks retired in 1930. He was said to have been an inarticulate teacher, but full of practical advice when he could be persuaded to utter.

Steer developed into a landscape painter of great power and originality. Bored with theories and discussion about art, he usually dropped off to sleep if anybody started to theorise. His instincts led him to marry the techniques of Constable to those of the Impressionists, and it is this mixture of qualities which makes some of his landscapes – including some in watercolour – consummate masterpieces. He also painted a handful of portraits of rare and delicate quality.

He was completely unlike the popular image of how an artist should look, in sharp contrast, for example, to Augustus John. He was a large, bow-fronted, placid, slow-moving, comfortable man, always dressed in subfusc clothes, and he greatly disliked any sort of display. He was careful, prudent, a cat-lover, and a bachelor, who quietly built up a fine collection of coins and who took quite extraordinary care of his health. Never a member of the Royal Academy, Steer does, however, number in that exclusive list of artists who have been awarded the Order of Merit, which he received in 1931 (it is said that he showed the medal to Tonks, saying, 'Have you got one of these?'). Soon after this his eyesight began to fail, an affliction which he faced with benign tolerance and fortitude. By the outbreak of World War II he had ceased to be able to work; he died in 1942.

Steer was one of a group of artists sent by the BWMC to ports on the south coast on behalf of the Royal Navy. Those concerned were naturally hoping for a really impressive picture from this master artist. Steer stayed for a month at Dover, having made an astonishing number of stipulations, insisting on shelter from the wind and the sun, demanding a nearby lavatory at all times, and requiring protection from inquisitive children. It must be doubted if Dover harbour was in fact a good subject for Steer (a good subject being another of his stipulations); certainly the pictures must have been something of a disappointment to the committee which had commissioned them.

* His house, duly marked with a blue plaque, is on Chelsea Embankment not far from Battersea Bridge.

GEORGE CLAUSEN's work for the BWMC was another large canvas – *In the Gun Factory at Woolwich Arsenal*.

This was a curious subject to have chosen for this artist, who was a *plein air* specialist. He was another Royal Academy heavyweight, having been made a full member of that body in 1908. He was born in 1852, the son of a Danish decorative painter who had emigrated to England. Clausen trained first at the South Kensington School, the institution which was to become the Royal College of Art in due course, and subsequently in Paris. As with so many other students, Whistler was a powerful influence, as were the Impressionists, especially Monet. Bastien-Lepage was another painter who left his mark on Clausen.

A founder-member of the New English Art Club, Clausen also taught at the Royal Academy Schools. He had devised his own style, which could be called semi-Impressionist. Like many of the original Impressionists, he preferred open-air subjects, especially in figure

Sir George Clausen, *Youth Mourning*
Oil, 36 × 36 ins
Dated 1916, and presented to the Imperial War Museum in 1929, this painting demonstrates the artist's personal response to the war, in sharp contrast to his official response (page 82).

Sir George Clausen, *In the Gun Factory at Woolwich Arsenal*
Oil, 72 × 125 ins
Another very large canvas, picturing Britain's foremost munitions factory.

painting, and this led him to scour the country for 'real peasant sub-jects'. Concentration on these subjects meant that in later years he could very easily be taken for an early social-realist painter. In fact he was interested not so much in the life of the rural poor as in the effects of light.

But he was a versatile and workmanlike artist, who was perfectly willing to turn his attention to the problems of painting a monumental picture such as that of Woolwich Arsenal. After the war, his career went on as it had in Edwardian days. He was knighted in 1927 and died, aged ninety-two, in 1944.

Though younger, HENRY RUSHBURY was an artist similar to Muirhead Bone – a traditional topographical draughtsman of great skill, an etcher and a watercolourist. He was born in 1889 into a lower-middle-class family in the Midlands, and studied art for six years at the Birmingham School of Art. He moved to London in 1912, where he learnt etching from Francis Dodd and found his real *métier*. In 1914 he joined the Royal Engineers as a draughtsman; in the same capacity he later transferred to the Royal Flying Corps, the predecessor of the Royal Air Force. By this time he was a sergeant. He did not go to France, but served in London throughout the war.

He was employed as an official war artist, as a general utility man in London. He produced a large number of etchings and drawings. Many of these had as their subjects the unusual sights to be seen in wartime London, such as the huts erected in St James's Park to house some of the additional civil servants, who overflowed the permanent government buildings of Whitehall; the allotments dug near Kensington Palace as part of the campaign to alleviate the food rationing caused, in the main, by the sinking of ships in the Atlantic by German U-boats; and the war refugees' camp in Earl's Court. Sometimes he was asked to record an event, such as a memorial service in St Paul's Cathedral. In all these pictures he showed his mastery of mood, a characteristic which he always retained, marking him as an artist of exceptional skill.

After the war, he had a spell at the Slade School in 1919. He then took up his career as an etcher and topographical artist, architectural and other subjects keeping him happily occupied for years, both in Britain and on the Continent. Made an RA in 1936, he also served as an official war artist in World War II. He became Keeper of the Royal Academy in 1949, holding this post until 1964, the year in which he was knighted. Pickwickian in appearance, he was a genial and engaging man, full of charm and good humour. He died in 1969.

BERNARD MENINSKY was born in 1891 of Jewish parents in the Ukraine; though he nearly missed this original birthplace, since his parents emigrated six weeks later, the pogroms forcing them to leave their homeland for Britain. They settled in Liverpool, and it was at the Liverpool School of Art that Bernard Meninsky began his studies in 1906. These were continued in Paris in 1911, and also at the Slade School in 1912 and 1913. He then had a year in Florence, working with the artist, stage-designer and writer Gordon Craig. He started teaching at the Central School as early as 1914.

He served as a private in the Royal Fusiliers, a London Regiment which attracted an unusual proportion of Jewish recruits. Three battalions of this regiment, mainly Jewish, formed a brigade in Allenby's army in Palestine. Allegedly their motto was 'No Advance Without Security'.

In his work as an official war artist, Bernard Meninsky concentrated on the dramatic and painfully heartrending scenes which occurred daily at the London railway termini. He recorded the arrivals at and departures from these places – battle-weary men arriving for a brief period of home leave and the unbearably poignant departures a few days later.

Bernard Meninsky was a versatile artist, a talented painter of figures and of landscapes in oils, gouache and watercolour. He was prominent in the London Group in the 1920s, also working in France and in Spain. He taught at Westminster School of Art from 1920, and at the City of Oxford Art School twenty years later. He died in London in 1950.

Another artist to be attracted to the platforms of the London stations was ALFRED HAYWARD, also employed as an official war artist in the closing months of the war. Born in London in 1875, he was another former Slade student, having attended that school from 1895 to 1897 after being at the Royal College of Art from 1891. He was a painter of

Sir Henry Rushbury, *St Paul's Cathedral – The Memorial Service to Captain Fryatt, July 1919*
Charcoal with touches of colour, 20½ × 15¾ ins
The rarely opened main doors of St Paul's Cathedral admit the cortège of Captain C. A. Fryatt, master of the SS *Brussels*, who was shot at Bruges by the Germans in July 1916.

Bernard Meninsky, *The Arrival*
Oil, 30 × 40 ins
A leave train has arrived at Victoria Station. Soldiers, some in the Balmorals worn
by Highland regiments, and all with their full kit and rifles, are saying a temporary
farewell to their friends before hurrying on to their homes. Mugs of tea are
available.

Alfred Hayward, *The Staff Train at Charing Cross Station*
Oil, 42 × 60 ins
Staff officers had many privileges, including, by 1918, a separate train to return them to France after leave or other visits to England. Boots and spurs were a normal feature of uniforms at this time; it is perfectly true that regulations forbade the wearing of spurs in observation balloons.

Bernard Meninsky, *On the Departure Platform*
Oil, 36 × 28 ins
Leave, traditionally pronounced 'leaf' in the army, is nearly over, ten days being the usual allotment. Here, soldiers of the Highland regiments, fully armed and equipped, assemble at Victoria Station to catch the leave train back to Dover and on to rejoin their units in France.

landscape, figures and portraits, and a supporter of the New English Art Club.

Joining the Artists' Rifles in 1914, at the age of thirty-nine, he was commissioned into the Royal Artillery two years later. As well as such pictures as *The Staff Train at Charing Cross Station*, as an official war artist he also painted portraits. He lived longer than any other artist mentioned in this book, dying in 1971 at the age of ninety-six.*

Those who were concerned with the planning for the Hall of Remembrance did not neglect the possibilities of sculpture. One of those who was commissioned to make a contribution was GILBERT LEDWARD who at the time, in 1918, was serving as a lieutenant in the Royal Artillery. He was asked to produce an enormous frieze, forty feet in length and large enough for life-size figures, the subject being the invasion of Belgium and the Battle of Mons. In fact this was never completed, but a preliminary design for it was finished.

Gilbert Ledward was born in Chelsea in 1888, the son of a sculptor. He had a prolonged training, lasting until 1914. This took place in successive colleges, at the Chelsea Polytechnic, Goldsmith's College, the Royal College of Art and the Royal Academy Schools. After the war he was busily occupied for many years with sculptured memorials in stone, the most prominent of these being the Guards' memorial on Horse Guards Parade. He taught for a few years in the 1920s at the Royal College of Art. He became an RA in 1937, and died in 1960.

* Are artists a long-lived lot? Ten per cent of those mentioned in this book lived into their nineties.

Gilbert Ledward, *18-pounder Gun in Action*
Plaster relief, 69 × 117 ins
A cast of a panel of the Guards Memorial on Horse Guards Parade. Eighteen-pounders were never operated by the Guards, being the preserve of the Royal Artillery.

C. SARGEANT JAGGER was also commissioned to produce a vast frieze for the Hall of Remembrance. As in Gilbert Ledward's case, this was never completed, although a preliminary design was: in Jagger's case the subject was *The First Battle of Ypres 1914: The Worcesters at Gheluvelt*. That this was the battle known in the army as First Ypres can be seen plainly in Jagger's design since the British troops are wearing peaked caps, which were used before steel helmets were supplied as an essential for trench warfare, where naturally head injuries were very frequent in the early days. Likewise the Germans are wearing the *pickelhaube*, the deco-

rated, spiked helmets which they wore before they, too, adopted the steel helmet. The British version resembled an inverted bowl, the German one being more like a miniature domestic coal-scuttle.

Charles Sargeant Jagger was born in Yorkshire, into a family of artists – he had a brother and a sister who were both painters. At first he worked in Sheffield for the famous firm of silversmiths, Mappin and Webb. He studied at the Sheffield School of Art before moving to London to study sculpture at the Royal College of Art from 1903 to 1910.

Like so many others mentioned in this book, Jagger joined the Artists' Rifles in 1914, being commissioned in the Worcestershire Regiment early in 1915. He served with the 5th Battalion of the Worcesters, in Gallipoli and subsequently on the Western Front. He was wounded no fewer than three times and was decorated for gallantry with the Military Cross.

Starting work as a sculptor in London in 1918, he too was occupied for many years with memorials; in his case the most prominent of these are the Royal Artillery memorial at Hyde Park Corner, and that at Paddington Station. (Not as well known as it should be, this powerful bronze, *Soldier Reading a Letter*, can still be seen on platform 1.) An ARA in 1926, he died young, only eight years later.

Nobody in authority in London, whether political or military, imagined that the war would end in 1918. It had been supposed that the American troops would have to built up to very large numbers before a military victory could be achieved; this was envisaged as occurring in 1919 or even 1920, by which time there would have been 5,000,000 American troops in France. The great successes of the British army from August 1918 onwards were as unexpected as they were welcome.

As soon as the Armistice was signed, it was instantly assumed tht there was no longer any need for propaganda. The Ministry of Information was wound up with promptitude, disappearing by the end of the year. The activities of the war artists were scarcely affected by this sudden change as the Imperial War Museum stepped in, but not before the whole concept of the Hall of Remembrance had been quietly shelved. This must be one of the very few occasions on which Lord Beaverbrook failed to achieve one of his aims. Nevertheless he had initiated the concept of acquiring paintings and other works of art not only for the immediate needs of propaganda (as these needs were perceived), but for posterity, as a permanent record.

Charles Sargeant Jagger, *The First Battle of Ypres, 1914: The Worcesters at Gheluvelt*
Plaster relief, 96 × 154 ins
Gheluvelt lies five miles south-east of Ypres, on the Menin road (N9). It was held at first by the British, but fell to the Germans at the end of October 1914.

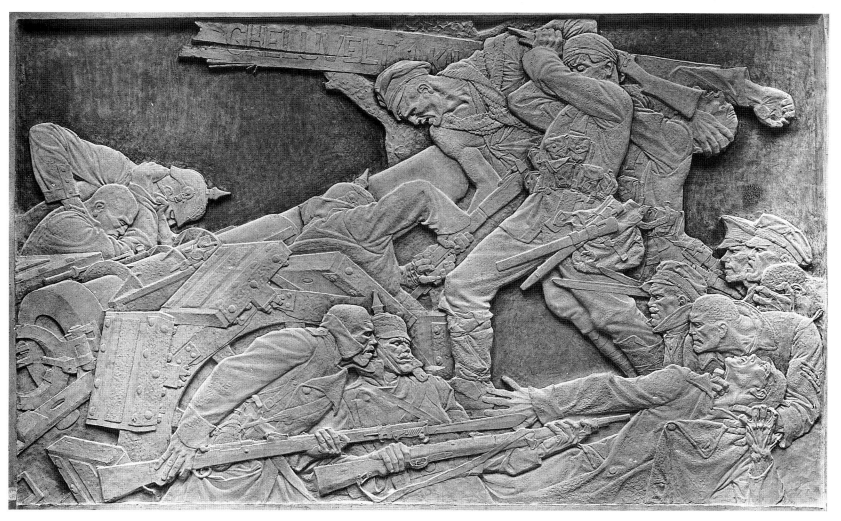

This had already become one of the objects of the Imperial War Museum. A museum of this kind had first been suggested in February 1917, by two men acting independently, both using the traditional method of writing an article for *The Times*. The two men were Charles ffoulkes, then the Curator of Armour at the Tower of London, and Ian Malcolm, the Conservative MP for Croydon. Malcolm was a relatively obscure backbencher; he never held office, except for a couple of years as a Parliamentary Private Secretary. He had married a daughter of the famous beauty Lily Langtrey in 1902 and had been associated briefly with Winston Churchill in the Tory ginger-group nicknamed 'the Hooligans'. Six years older than Churchill, he lived until 1944. The suggestions of Ian Malcolm and of Charles ffoulkes were seized on by Sir Alfred Mond, the First Commissioner of Works, head of the government department which was later to become the Ministry of Works.

Mond was born in 1868 (as, curiously enough, were both Malcolm and ffoulkes); he was of German-Jewish origin and was later to become the first Lord Melchett. He was the son of the co-founder of the chemical firm of Brunner, Mond, which also made explosives; when this business was amalgamated with others in the 1920s to form Imperial Chemical Industries, Alfred Mond became its first chairman. He was a Liberal MP from 1906, switching to the Conservative side in 1924. He was a forceful, unpopular man. Appointed First Commissioner of Works in 1916, he was far more of a businessman than a politician. His department had the enormous task, amongst many others, of finding convenient accommodation in London for the greatly swollen wartime Civil Service. The First Commissioner's post, politically a low-grade appointment, similar in those days to that of postmaster-general, was exactly the sort of job liable to be given to somebody with a business background, especially in wartime. Mond was a wealthy man, and a collector of art, amongst other things.

When the new museum was formed it had ffoulkes on its staff and Malcolm on its supervising committee, which also included representatives from each of the services who were charged with the duty of acquiring suitable material for preservation. This duty was seen, from the first, to include the purchase and the commissioning of paintings and sculpture. In December 1917 Robert Ross was appointed honorary art adviser.

Ross, who also advised the BWMC on art, is best known today as the man who befriended Oscar Wilde, stood by him when he came out of prison, looked after him in his voluntary exile in Paris, became a most capable literary executor to the Wilde estate, and commissioned Wilde's Paris gravestone from the young Jacob Epstein. He was a Canadian who had lived in London for many years. A journalist and, later, a picture-dealer, he was a trustee of the National Gallery and adviser to the Inland Revenue on picture valuations for estate duty. He was very well known in literary and artistic circles, and attended all exhibitions as they came along. He was to buy many pictures for the Imperial War Museum.

The Imperial War Museum did its utmost to buy pictures covering every single facet of the war; one large aspect was veterinary. It must be recalled that the great majority of transport during the war involved horses. Throughout the conflict ordinary infantry battalions at the front had no mechanical transport of any kind on their 'establishment'. Horses were, of course, never seen in the trenches, but the more senior officers of the unit would ride their chargers on the line of march.* There were many cavalry units, albeit often operating dismounted. Thousands of guns and wagons were hauled by draught horses. On both sides, scores of thousands of horses were involved; they all needed veterinary attention. The German army, apart from the mobile and armoured Panzer divisions, required large numbers of horses for these purposes throughout World War *II*.

These veterinary aspects were one of the subjects covered by THOMAS CANTRELL DUGDALE, a versatile painter who had the necessary special knowledge. He was an exception in that he was a Territorial soldier who had joined the Middlesex Yeomanry, a territorial cavalry regiment, in 1910. He served in the ranks of this unit throughout the war, ending it with the rank of squadron sergeant-major. The Middlesex Yeomanry went with the Yeomanry Division to the Middle East, just as this same division was to do in World War II. It saw service at Gallipoli and in Palestine, almost the only fighting front where cavalry actually operated as cavalry traditionally had for centuries past. Dugdale recorded one such occasion in the only picture of a cavalry charge in the museum's collection – *Charge of the 2nd Lancers at El Afuli, Palestine*.

Born in Blackburn in 1880, T. C. Dugdale had first trained at the Manchester School of Art, moving on to the Royal College of Art, the City and Guilds School and to the Académie Julian in Paris. He was a portrait and subject painter, a decorative painter and a designer of textiles. Appointed an RA in 1936, he died in 1952.

The first artist to be commissioned by the Imperial War Museum was ADRIAN HILL. His route towards his appointment was unusual. Born in 1895, he was a student at the Royal College of Art before joining the Honourable Artillery Company (HAC), the City of London Territorial unit which has the longest history in the country as a volunteer force. Hill joined up in 1914. He served for three years in the ranks of the HAC, which was the first Territorial unit to go to France, and was

* When first commissioned in 1941, my own commanding officer used to appear on parade on a charger he had somehow wangled; this was not thought to be more than mildly eccentric.

T. C. Dugdale, *Charge of the 2nd Lancers at El Afuli, Palestine*
Oil, 28 × 36 ins
The 2nd Lancers, an Indian regiment commanded at the time by a captain, charged a Turkish position on 20 September 1918, killing fifty and taking 500 prisoners, for the loss of one man wounded and twelve horses killed. El Afuli is on the railway line, some thirty miles south-east of Haifa.

Adrian Hill, 'A Penny all the Way'
Ink and watercolour, 12¼ × 17¼ ins
Commandeered London buses near Amiens, a town which remained in Allied hands throughout the war.

encouraged to draw and sketch by his commanding officer, who had in mind illustrations for the regimental history which would be compiled in due course.

When invalided back to Britain in 1917 Hill showed some of these drawings to the authorities of the recently established museum. He was promptly commissioned as a second lieutenant and appointed an official war artist. Sent back to France, he was posted to the new War Trophies Section at General Headquarters, which was already working closely with the museum, assembling suitable material for future display. Hill spent the remaining months of the war at this work, producing a very large number of drawings. These give a vivid, journalistic record of military life in all its ramifications, though Hill was dealing mainly with subjects in the rear areas.

Adrian Hill's style was not unlike that of Muirhead Bone, though he did not match the latter's skill in finding telling viewpoints. Hill was a competent artist, painstaking, accurate and hard-working. He found recognition as a teacher of painting techniques in a series of television programmes.

The 'establishment' of the War Trophies Section at GHQ in France allowed for two artists. The Imperial War Museum's nomination for the second of these posts was a very bold one indeed: it was none other than JACOB EPSTEIN, at the time the most controversial sculptor in Britain. Later, of course, he was to become the most distinguished sculptor in the country, before the emergence of Henry Moore.

Epstein was born in New York in 1880, into a well-to-do family of Orthodox Jews, immigrants from Poland and Russia. He studied art in his native city and began to make his way there as an artist. With fees he had earned from illustrating a book, he was able to travel to Paris. Here he studied again, at the Beaux-Arts and at the Académie Julian, and spent much time in museums studying the sculpture of the past, and also assimilating ideas from Mexico, from Africa and from Buddhist carving.

In 1905 he came to London armed with a letter of introduction from Rodin, addressed to Bernard Shaw; Shaw did his best for the younger man, introducing him to his artist friends such as the highly influential William Rothenstein and Robert Ross. Epstein liked London so much that he became a naturalised citizen of Britain in 1911.

Adrian Hill, An Advanced Cage for German Prisoners
Ink and watercolour, 19½ × 15½ ins
Dejection and resignation are equally apparent. These men were not yet free from danger, as they could still be used in the forward areas on such tasks as carrying wounded on stretchers to dressing stations.

Another influential friend, Francis Dodd, had introduced Epstein to the architect Charles Holden (who was later to produce abortive plans for the Hall of Remembrance). This introduction led to the first public uproar which engulfed the hapless sculptor, in 1908. Holden commissioned from Epstein eighteen large figures, rather more than lifesize. Carved in Portland stone, these figures were to flank the second-floor windows of the new building in the Strand which Holden had designed as the new headquarters of the British Medical Association, the ruling body for the medical profession. Naturally enough, in the circumstances, the figures were nudes, depicting men and women in all stages of life from birth to old age. When the scaffolding was removed from the building and the public could see the figures, appalling clamour erupted. Sculptured nude figures had been, of course, part of civilised life from the time of the ancient Greeks; it is therefore very puzzling to try to understand this uproar today. It is true that Epstein's figures were large, and it is true that eighteen figures are rather different from a single figure, and it is true that all the figures were in Epstein's uncompromising and uninhibited style. But they are high up and, as the building is on a corner site, it is not easy to see all the figures at once. The building is certainly a prominent one, the style of the sculptures was new to Britain, and Epstein was still an American citizen at the time. All these factors may have played a part. The BMA took a robust attitude and did nothing to appease the philistine outburst.

But the doctors grew out of the building in due course, and they moved to larger premises in Bloomsbury in the 1930s. The Strand building was then taken over by the Southern Rhodesian government, to house its High Commission; it was the commission which proceeded to vandalise and ruin Epstein's work*, causing more uproar, this time from a different standpoint. Sickert resigned from the Royal Academy in 1935 because of the equivocal attitude of that body to this act of desecration.

It is even more difficult for us to understand today the similar fracas which developed in Paris, of all places, in 1911. Oscar Wilde had died in Paris in 1900, and was buried there in the Père Lachaise cemetery. In 1910 a memorial tombstone was commissioned from Epstein; when this was unveiled another puritan outburst ensued. The authorities insisted that a fig-leaf should be added to conceal the genitals of an angel which is the main feature of the memorial. In due course a night-time raid by young artists removed the fig-leaf.

Epstein's stone carvings seemed always to arouse controversy, the public finding his bronzes far more readily acceptable. Even his *Rima*, a memorial to the naturalist W. H. Hudson in Hyde Park, caused violent dissension when it was first seen in 1925: looking at it today it is impossible to imagine what the fuss could possibly have been about.

The Tin Hat, one of Epstein's bronzes, had a great success when shown at a London exhibition in 1917. The sculptor was serving as a

* The mutilated figures, with heads, limbs and so on chiselled off, can be seen to this day, since the building has survived otherwise intact. Now called Zimbabwe House, it is on the north side of the Strand, on the corner of Agar Street.

Sir Jacob Epstein, *Sergeant D. F. Hunter, VC*
Bronze, 23½ ins
Sergeant Hunter's Victoria Cross was won as a corporal in the 1/5th Highland Light Infantry and was gazetted on 23 October 1918.

private in the Royal Fusiliers, in England, and the success of *The Tin Hat* prompted the museum authorities to arrange for Epstein's appointment as an official war artist. But his appointment to the vacant post in France did not materialise because of objections which were raised. Robert Ross was an enthusiastic Epstein supporter; indeed it was Ross who had commissioned the Wilde memorial (in which Ross himself was later buried as well). But Ross's recommendation was overridden, for reasons which cannot now be established – possibly because of the undoubtedly controversial style of Epstein's work,

Sir Jacob Epstein, *An American Soldier*
Bronze, 15¾ ins
British-style steel helmets were issued to American troops. The USA had declared war on 2 April 1917.

Sir Jacob Epstein, *Admiral of the Fleet Lord Fisher of Kilverstone, GCB, OM, GCVO*
Bronze, 18½ ins
Fisher had ended his term as First Sea Lord in 1910, but was recalled to this post in October 1914, resigning in May 1915. He was a tempestuous personality, known both as 'Jackie' and as 'the old Malay'.

possibly because of his American origins, perhaps even for anti-Semitic reasons: we shall never know.

The portrait heads by Epstein in the museum's collection were presented by the ever-generous Muirhead Bone. They have the powerful and masterly qualities which are associated with his work, and it is a matter of regret that there are not more of them.

The artist went on, of course, to a career of the utmost distinction. His most prominent works are the *Christ in Majesty* in Llandaff Cathedral; his *St Michael and the Devil* on an outside wall of Coventry Cathedral; *Night* and *Day* on the London Transport office building above St James's Park Underground station (another building designed by Charles Holden); and the modestly sized but potent *Madonna and Child* on the Holy Child Convent on the north side of Cavendish Square.

Epstein was an occasional painter and illustrator, a generous patron of younger artists (Moore, for example), and a collector. His personal collection was given by his widow to the Walsall Art Gallery in 1973; the artist himself, knighted in 1954, had died in 1959.

Glyn Philpot, *Admiral of the Fleet Sir John Jellicoe, GCB, OM, GCVO*
Oil, 50 × 40 ins
Jellicoe commanded the Grand Fleet from 4 August 1914 until he was appointed First Sea Lord in December 1916, remaining in that post only twelve months.

Perhaps because of the navy's long tradition of employing artists with the fleet, usually to paint battle scenes, the naval authorities took especial pains to ensure that the work done under their auspices was of high quality. It was for naval purposes that Steer had been commissioned, and he was widely regarded by expert opinion as the most distinguished artist in Britain. Quality was also in mind when GLYN PHILPOT was commissioned to paint portraits of admirals; these were not to be drawings, such as Francis Dodd had already produced, but full-blown portraits in oils.

At the time, this was an adventurous choice of artist. Philpot was born in London in 1884, the son of a surveyor of strict Lutheran persuasion. He trained at the Lambeth School of Art, where he was taught by Philip Connard, his senior by nine years, and at the Académie Julian. After a visit to Spain in 1909, he had some success in London as a painter of genre, and of religious, mythological and allegorical subjects. In 1913 he went to America, painting portraits for the first time. He was painting in Venice in August 1914, but hurried back to Britain to enlist. Commissioned in the Royal Army Service Corps, Philpot was later invalided out of the army.

His skill as a portrait painter was not recognised in London when he was selected to paint the admirals; but later he was to become very well known in this field, renowned for his facility and his brilliant, luminous palette. In fact he found the admirals a very difficult lot, as sitters. He was irked to discover that they could not spare the time to visit his studio, and he found the working conditions that he was obliged to adopt very tiresome. As a result he finished only four portraits.

Glyn Philpot also painted one of the murals in St Stephen's Hall (as can be seen briefly by visitors to the House of Commons), and was appointed an RA in 1923. He died, aged fifty-three, in 1937.

A second distinguished artist used by the naval authorities to paint portraits was AMBROSE MCEVOY.

His was an unusual background, bordering on the exotic. His father was an Irish-American mercenary soldier, or soldier of fortune as it was described at the time. He had served in the Confederate forces in the American Civil War. At some point his wounds were treated by a doctor, with whom he struck up a close friendship. This was Doctor Whistler, a brother of the artist James Abbott McNeill Whistler. At the end of the American Civil War both the doctor and the patient moved to Britain, while maintaining their friendship.

Ambrose McEvoy was born in 1878, and showed skill as an artist while a boy. By this date, J. A. M. Whistler was a highly influential and much-respected artist, oscillating between London and Paris. He advised the budding McEvoy to enrol at the Slade School; this was done when McEvoy was only fifteen. Later he worked with Sickert in Dieppe. He became known for his poetical landscapes, his restful interiors and for his admirable portraits, especially of women.

McEvoy completed nineteen naval portraits for the Imperial War Museum, including a number of holders of the Victoria Cross. To achieve this he had to spend much time with the Grand Fleet, a three-month period on the Western Front with the Royal Naval Division,* and a vexatious time doing his best to create from photographs portraits of men to whom the VC had been awarded posthumously.

After the war, McEvoy resumed his portrait-painting career. Like his counterpart Glyn Philpot, he died young. He was only forty-nine when he died in 1927.

CHARLES PEARS (1873–1958) was another artist who did a great deal of naval work for the Imperial War Museum, which holds ninety-nine of his pictures from World War I (he was also to be a naval artist in World War II). Pears was a specialist marine painter, experienced in this field and very conscientious. Much of his work was done in Harwich, or in ships which operated from Harwich; he also worked in Rosyth, and with the Grand Fleet at Scapa Flow.

Another prolific artist who was attached to the Royal Navy was PHILIP CONNARD, a teacher, an illustrator, and a painter of portraits, landscapes and decorative designs. Connard was another artist who had made his own way. Born in Southport in 1875, he started life as a house-painter and decorator, but went to night-school for lessons in art. Persistence rewarded him with a scholarship to the Royal College

* The Royal Naval Division was hastily created in the early days of the war, drawn mainly from naval reservists who had been called up but for whom the navy, although vast in size, could find no seagoing employment. The division served in Antwerp, at Gallipoli and in France. Many well-known people served as officers in this force which was, to some extent, a private army of the First Lord of the Admiralty. These included George Cornwallis-West, Churchill's former stepfather, then married to the actress Mrs Patrick Campbell, and Rupert Brooke, a friend of Churchill's secretary Eddie Marsh.

Glyn Philpot, *Dame Katherine Furse, CBE, RRC*
Oil, 24 × 30 ins
After work as a Voluntary Aid Detachment (volunteer nursing) organiser in France and London, Dame Katherine became the first director of the Women's Royal Naval Service when it was started in November 1917.

Ambrose McEvoy, *Commander D. M. W. Beak, VC, DSO, MC, RNVR*
Oil, 40 × 30 ins
Joining the Royal Naval Volunteer Reserve as a seaman, Commander Beak was made a sub-lieutenant in May 1915 and was posted to the Royal Naval Division, serving in Gallipoli and in France. By March 1917 he was commanding a battalion. His VC was gazetted on 15 November 1918.

of Art, and he also studied at the Académie Julian in Paris. He established himself as an artist in London, and also taught at the Lambeth School of Art, where his pupils included Glyn Philpot.

When war came he enlisted, and rose to the rank of captain in the Royal Artillery. He worked as an artist with the navy from 1916. Much

Charles Pears, *A Convoy*
Oil, 30 × 51 ins
Although convoys of merchant shipping had been used with success in the Napoleonic wars, the Admiralty was reluctant to organise them in the earlier days of the war, apart from in special cases and for troop movements. They were started, at Lloyd George's insistence, in May 1917, with immediate and successful results.

of his work, and there are eighty pictures of his in the Imperial War Museum, was concerned with operations in the North Sea. However, he was in the Mediterranean at the end of the war, recording, amongst other things, the surrender in Constantinople of the German cruiser *Goeben*, the vessel whose arrival in that city had done so much to create the alliance between Germany and Turkey.

Appointed an RA in 1925, he served as Keeper twenty years later for a four-year period. He died in 1958.

Ambrose McEvoy, *Bourlon Wood*
Oil, 25 × 30 ins
Bourlon is five miles due west of Cambrai. It was nearly taken by the British in November 1917 in the course of fighting in which tanks were used with great success, some 500 being engaged. Bourlon Wood eventually fell in September 1918, with the Royal Naval Division taking a major role.

NORMAN WILKINSON was also a naval artist. Already very well known as a marine artist by the outbreak of the war, he was older than many of his colleagues – he was born in 1878. He was commissioned into the Royal Naval Volunteer Reserve (familiarly known as the Wavy Navy, since the gold bands on officers' sleeves which indicated their rank were waved rather than straight); Wilkinson achieved the rank of lieutenant-commander, the naval equivalent of an army major. He became famous as the man who first thought of dazzle-painting for ships.

Norman Wilkinson, *The Base Camp, Cape Helles, under Shell Fire, August 1915*
Oil, 24 × 36 ins
The vessel on the left is the beached *River Clyde*. On the first day of the Gallipoli landings, the 1,500 men on the *River Clyde* had incurred 1,200 casualties.

Philip Connard, *The Guns of HMS* Caesar
Oil, 20 × 24 ins
Painted in 1918, after the Allies had occupied Constantinople. HMS *Caesar*, a Majestic-class battleship dating from 1896, mounted 12-inch guns.

Philip Connard, *27 Knots: HMS* Melampus
Oil, 28 × 36 ins
HMS *Melampus* was a 1,040-ton destroyer. At the beginning of the war she was being built for the Greek Navy on the Clyde, but she was at once purchased for the Royal Navy. She sank a U-boat off Selsea Bill on the Sussex coast in October 1917.

Norman Wilkinson, *Troops landing at C Beach, Suvla Bay, 7 August 1915*
Oil, 24 × 36 ins
Initially there was little opposition to the landings in Suvla Bay; but the advantage thus gained was not vigorously exploited, and Turkish resistance soon stiffened.

The idea behind this concept was part of the anti-U-boat campaign. When a U-boat encountered an Allied ship, the course and speed had to be deduced before torpedoes could be fired with any chance of success. Working out this calculation was, naturally, never easy, as the ship could only be observed briefly in a series of rapid glimpses through the U-boat's periscope. The hazards of weather were apt to make the task more difficult. And it was believed that dazzle-painting – painting a ship in different colours, for camouflage – would make it more difficult again, especially at night. So ships were all disguised in blocks of contrasting colours, in an unintentionally Cubist style.

Norman Wilkinson had been at Gallipoli, which began as a purely naval attack, and in fact was highly ineffective. He recorded the landing at Suvla Bay, and the considerable naval activity in the area, in a brilliant series of watercolour sketches. He had great skill and much experience, and these small pictures have an intense liveliness and spontaneity.

Wilkinson resumed his career as a maritime artist after the war, never straying far from the territory which he had mastered so completely. He was awarded the CBE in 1948; another long-lived artist, he died in 1971.

RONALD GRAY (1868–1951) specialised in pictures of the newly invented technique of anti-aircraft gunnery, established in London as a form of defence against bombing raids by Zeppelins. He served as an able seaman in the Royal Naval Volunteer Reserve, and seemed content to 'do his bit' in this humble role. He was born in Chelsea. His father was a heating engineer who must have been something of a pioneer as central heating was in its infancy in the 1860s. Ronald Gray worked briefly in the family business, leaving it for the Westminster School of Art and the Académie Julian. He became a figure and landscape painter in oils and watercolour. He was a follower and a friend of Wilson Steer, although he never had the benefit of his teaching at the Slade, where Steer was on the staff for so many years.

Another painter who is very well represented – by more than fifty works – in the naval section of the museum's collection is FRANK MASON (1876–1965). He was a marine painter in oils and watercolour, an illustrator and a poster-designer. Self-taught, he had exhibited at the Royal Academy from 1900. Commissioned as a lieutenant in the Royal Naval Volunteer Reserve, he served throughout the war in the North Sea and in Egyptian waters.

Naval activity was also recorded, in more than a hundred works in the museum's collection, by DONALD MAXWELL (1877–1936). A marine and landscape painter, he had trained at the Slade and had started to exhibit at the Royal Academy in 1906. He had served in the navy as a lieutenant, Royal Naval Volunteer Reserve, before becoming an official war artist for the Admiralty. Subsequently he travelled to Palestine and Mesopotamia for the museum. Most of his work in the museum is concerned with naval activity in the Mediterranean.

Naval matters were also the concern of L. CAMPBELL TAYLOR (1874–1969). He served in the army until 1917, eventually as a captain in the Surrey Volunteer Regiment, before transferring to the navy in the equivalent rank of lieutenant, Royal Naval Volunteer Reserve. He was a painter of genre, portraits and interiors with figures, rather than a specialist marine painter. Born in Oxford, he had trained there at the Ruskin School before moving to the St John's Wood School and then to the Royal Academy Schools in 1905, having exhibited at the Academy from 1899. He was appointed an RA in 1931.

JOHN WHEATLEY (1892–1955) was one of those artists who was extracted from the army to work as a war artist for the Royal Navy; more than fifty of the pictures he produced in this capacity are to be found in the museum's collection. A painter of portraits and genre, and an etcher, he was born in Abergavenny. He had trained with Stanhope Forbes, with Sickert and at the Slade School in the immediate pre-war years. He enlisted in 1914 and was serving as a sergeant in the Artists' Rifles when he was transferred to work for the Navy. He taught at the Slade in the post-war years before taking up a teaching post in South Africa, where he was to become director of the National Gallery of South Africa. He returned to Britain in 1938 to become director of the Sheffield City Art Gallery, where he succeeded the younger John Rothenstein.

Another remarkable artist used by the Royal Navy was J. D. FERGUSSON. Like Lamb and Tonks, he had abandoned the study of medicine for art. Fergusson was a Highlander born in 1874, and studied in Edinburgh and in Paris. Inspired, like so many others, by Whistler, and later by the painters of the Glasgow School, he settled in Paris in 1905; here he came under the influence of the Fauves, and was indeed the most distinguished British artist to be so influenced. Between 1910 and 1920 or thereabouts, he developed his own style, which parallels the Expressionism developing in Germany during this same period. In the inter-war years, Fergusson was loosely associated with the Scottish Colourists group.

Ronald Gray, *King's Cross Anti-aircraft Gun in Action*
Oil, 30 × 25 ins
Anti-aircraft gunfire was, naturally, a brand-new skill. Here it is being practised by Royal Navy gunners.

Frank Mason *The Air Raid on El Arish*
Watercolour, 9½ × 20 ins
Painted at Port Said, this picture records an extraordinary incident which occurred on 16 June 1916. In a raid on El Arish, on the Mediterranean coast of Sinai, a Royal Flying Corps pilot was obliged to force-land on the beach. Two colleagues in a BE2c saw what had happened and landed alongside. The damaged plane was set on fire, and all three officers successfully took off again.

Frank Mason, *The Mails Office: Ismailia*
Watercolour, 12 × 15½ins
The Indian Expeditionary Force Post Office at Ismailia, on the Suez Canal. Ismailia became familiar to many troops during and after World War II, when it was a centre for the British troops in the Canal Zone.

Donald Maxwell, *'St George for England'*
Pen and watercolour, 10¾ × 13¼ ins
British sea-planes bombing Ramleh, then in Turkish hands, on 23 December 1916. Ramleh, or Ramle, ten miles south-east of Tel Aviv, is the traditional birthplace of St George.

In World War I, the battle in the air was a completely novel aspect of fighting. During the early days, aeroplanes were thought of on both sides as a means of scouting and observing ahead of the troops on the ground. The pilots were unarmed. When trench warfare began, this function of aeroplanes was continued, with both sides doing their best to discover what was going on beyond the enemy's front line, which was all that could be seen on the ground. Captive balloons tethered at the front line, which were also sometimes used and often in concert with long-range artillery, could not see very much further. But aeroplanes could penetrate for miles.

Then aeroplanes began to dispute their own territory and the aptly named dog-fights began; at first with hand-held weapons, then with automatic weapons fired by a gunner, and finally with machine-guns of great sophistication which fired bullets timed to avoid the aeroplane's own whirring propeller. As aeroplanes grew in size and scope, the bombing of enemy targets began. And bombing of civilian targets, such

L. Campbell Taylor, *Herculaneum Dock, Liverpool*
Pen and watercolour, 11½ × 8½ ins
The ship in the foreground has an early form of camouflage; it was gradually superseded by the type displayed by the other two ships.

L CAMPBELL TAYLOR.
1918

John Wheatley, *Divers at Work, Repairing a Torpedoed Ship*
Oil, 42 × 60 ins
Forty per cent of the British merchant fleet was sunk in World War I. With losses
on this scale, the repair of damaged ships was a matter of the utmost importance.

John D. Fergusson, *Portsmouth Docks, 1918*
Oil, 29½ × 26½ ins
One of the fascinating aspects of this painting is the way in which the ships'
camouflage has been fitted into the highly individual composition.

Richard Carline, *Jerusalem and the Dead Sea from an Aeroplane*
Oil, 41½ × 51½ ins

By the end of the war the Allied forces in Palestine numbered 500,000. The task of keeping these numbers supplied is vividly brought to mind by Carline's bird's-eye view.

as that of London by Zeppelins, began as early as September 1915.

Naturally, the problems of recording the war in the air were even more difficult than those met with on the ground or at sea. Those pictures which were painted under official auspices were, on the whole, disappointing. There were many reasons for this, not the least of which was the fact that the Royal Air Force did not achieve its separate status and identity until April 1918. Before that date all flying was done by the Royal Naval Air Service and by the Royal Flying Corps. Both were, of course, very small parts of much larger organisations.

Two of the most effective artists of the war in the air were brothers, SYDNEY and RICHARD CARLINE. Richard was the younger, born in 1896. He was to be a post-war student at the Slade School. He enlisted and served in the Royal Flying Corps, first as an air-gunner, and subsequently as an airborne artist, first in France and then in the Middle East, where he was sent on a post-war tour with his brother.

Sydney Carline was eight years older than his brother. He had trained at the Slade from 1907 and later in Paris, and was to establish himself as a landscape painter, a portrait painter, an etcher and a designer of medals. He too served in the Royal Flying Corps, but as a pilot, an extremely hazardous form of service, given the primitive nature of the aeroplanes of the day.

The two brothers completed their tour of the Middle East and its battlefields, or battle-space, in November 1919. Post-war financial cuts were already biting, and the Imperial War Museum was able to acquire only a small amount of the Carlines' output. The brothers had the fortunate compensation, however, of being able to put on in March 1920 a private exhibition of the many pictures left in their possession, and this brought them both much public recognition and acclaim.

Later, Sydney Carline went on to provide illustrations for T. E. Lawrence's *Revolt in the Desert*. He died in 1929; his brother survived him by more than fifty years, dying in 1980.

Sydney Carline, *The Destruction of the Turkish Transport*
Oil, 48 × 48 ins
In the gorge of Wadi Fara, Palestine. On 21 September 1918, Turkish troops, almost surrounded as they tried to escape from the Nablus area towards the Jordan valley, were ruthlessly attacked by British aeroplanes, including the SE5s shown in this picture.

In wartime, governments everywhere ignore all the usual financial constraints. Money is found to pay for whatever is required; this is done not only by severe taxation but also by borrowing, often in the form of war bonds, a type of moral blackmail in which patriotic citizens are made to feel obliged to lend their money to the government at disadvantageous terms. All wars are horrendously expensive; in the wartime atmosphere, with normal prudent financing set aside, all sorts of expenditure seems justified, and not merely expenditure directly connected with the war effort.

But as soon as the conflict stops, the Treasury reasserts itself and soon climbs back into its usual powerful position, all the more so in that by then there is usually a very large additional debt to be paid.

This procedure was followed precisely in Britain after World War I. In 1919 those involved at the Imperial War Museum were soon obliged to face up to cuts in expenditure. Money had to be spread very thinly,

where previously it had not seemed to matter much. Compromises were made, where earlier they would not have been considered. Gifts of pictures were accepted, when they might well have been refused in other circumstances. Muirhead Bone most unselfishly sought to alleviate the situation by establishing a Bone Fund (to which he contributed £2,000) for the purchase of work which might otherwise have been lost to the museum.

A very large exhibition of pictures from the museum's collection opened in mid-December 1919. This idea attracted general critical approval. But the nature of the exhibition also attracted the popular press, who raised a not-unexpected furore about much of the modern work. This plainly bewildered the reporters sent to the press show, since many of them had not seen anything of the kind before – apart from an exhibition of Canadian pictures two years earlier, modern work was excluded from the Royal Academy, and appeared only at

modest shows in relatively small private galleries. The reporters concerned were able to enjoy themselves with much righteous indignation about the supposed freakishness of the pictures, the insults to 'our gallant dead' and so on. General, as opposed to informed, public taste was not ready for the sort of shocks that many of the younger artists had provided.

Described, not unfairly, as the most neglected English artist of his time, DAVID BOMBERG (1890–1957) is another artist represented in the Imperial War Museum as a result of the generosity of Muirhead Bone. Bomberg's work is extraordinary. He was involved with Vorticism as a young man, but developed into a powerful landscape painter, whose work was to become very influential among other artists.

David Bomberg, *Sappers at Work*
Charcoal, 26½ × 22 ins
A Canadian Tunnelling Company at St Eloi, about five miles north-west of Arras. Field-Marshal Wavell used to describe the trench warfare on the Western Front as a form of siege warfare. Sapping (digging tunnels under the enemy) and mining (blowing up enemy positions with explosives) played a part in this, just as they had done in eighteenth-century sieges.

David Bomberg was born in Birmingham into a family of émigré Polish Jews; his father was a craftsman in leatherwork. During his childhood the family moved to London, his father becoming involved in work for such shops as Asprey's. Bomberg studied at the City and Guild School, at the Westminster School of Art, at the Slade School and in Paris. He was a founder-member of the London Group. He served in the Royal Engineers from 1915 to 1918. Deeply affected by the war, in which a brother was killed in France, he was unable to paint at the time. But he had started to exhibit before the war, and it is very fortunate that his work came to the notice of the perceptive and knowledgeable Muirhead Bone, who appreciated Bomberg's powerful imagination and skill.

WALTER BAYES (1869–1956) is represented in the museum by only a small handful of paintings, but they are paintings of quality. At the time of the war he was a well-established artist, a painter of figures, landscapes and decorative work, and an illustrator. Born into a family of artists, he began his artistic education with evening classes at the City and Guilds Technical College in Finsbury, before attending the Westminster School of Art full-time at the turn of the century, when he had

Walter Bayes, *The Underworld*
Oil, 100 × 216 ins
Civilians taking cover in the Elephant and Castle Underground station. The first air raid on London occurred on 13 June 1917. In all, there were over a hundred air raids on Britain during the war, with 1,500 people killed and over 400 injured.

already been exhibiting at the Royal Academy for ten years. A founder-member of both the Camden Town and the London Groups, he was also a writer of books and a journalist – he was the art critic of the well-known and influential monthly *The Athenaeum* for ten years from 1906. Immediately after the war he became head of the Westminster School of Art, holding the post for sixteen years. During World War II he came out of retirement to teach painting at Lancaster School of Arts and Crafts.

FRANK BRANGWYN (1867–1956) has the extraordinary and unique distinction, for a British artist, of having not one but two museums devoted to his work on the Continent: one at Orange, in southern France, the other at Bruges, his Belgian birthplace. Brangwyn, whose father was a Welsh architect, built up a worldwide reputation as a decorative artist, his large murals with many figures being executed in brilliant colours. Many of his murals are to be seen in notable buildings in Britain and in the United States. An ARA in 1904, he advanced to RA in 1919 and was knighted in 1941. His reputation also embraced his work as an etcher and a lithographer.

At first a neutral country, Italy had been persuaded to join the Allies in 1915 by tempting offers of territory to be allocated to her when the war was over. For two years Italy was locked in conflict with Austria in the mountainous borders of those two countries. It was a limited, almost a private war. But its character changed in October 1917 when additional German forces, added to those of Austria, inflicted a stunning defeat on the Italians at the Battle of Caporetto. The Italians were obliged to retreat for eighty miles or more, and their army lost more than 800,000 men killed, wounded or taken prisoner. French and British troops were hurried to Italy to boost the bruised Italians.

The Italians were not able to do a great deal to supply official artists on this additional front during the remainder of the war. The museum was fortunate to find that the distinguished landscape painter R. G. BRUNDRIT (1883–1960) had served there as a driver of a Red Cross ambulance; five pictures of his are in the museum's collection. Reginald George Brundrit was another product of the Slade School. He was well regarded as a landscape painter, becoming an RA in 1938.

Today it seems as though qualifications, of one sort or another, are all-important to a career. It is extraordinary, and indeed salutary, for us to contemplate the career of CHARLES HOLMES, two of whose works are in the museum's collection. His was a career of the greatest possible distinction, yet he had no formal training or qualifications either as an artist or as an art historian and administrator.

Born in Preston, in comfortable circumstances, he went to Brasenose College, Oxford. From 1895 he worked in a London publishing house. It was at this time that he started exhibiting pictures at the New English

Sir Frank Brangwyn, *The Gun*
Lithograph, 18 × 14¼ ins
One of a series of lithographs entitled 'Britain's Efforts and Ideals'.

Reginald G. Brundrit, *The Carso Front, with Ruined Farm*
Pastel, 13¾ × 19 ins
The Carso area lies north-west of Trieste. It was lost to the Allies after the successful German-led attack at Caporetto in October 1917.

Sir Charles Holmes, *Awaiting Zeppelins, Sandringham, January 1915*
Oil 27 × 30 ins
Two Zeppelins dropped bombs in Norfolk on the night of 19/20 January 1915. Bombs landed in King's Lynn, killing two people and injuring thirteen. Great Yarmouth was also bombed.

Sir Herbert Hughes-Stanton, *The Lens–Arras Road*
Oil, 20 × 27 ins
The road from Arras to Lens (N25) passes across the Vimy Ridge, captured by the
Canadians in 1917. Hughes-Stanton's landscape, from the ridge, shows the village
of Vimy in the middle distance, to the right.

Art Club; as an artist he was entirely self-taught. He also wrote a good deal, producing both books and articles for newspapers and magazines. This led to his appointment in 1903 as the first editor of the *Burlington*; he held that influential post for six years. The following year he was appointed Slade Professor of Art at Oxford for a six-year term. In 1909 he became director of the National Portrait Gallery, moving round the corner in 1916 to become director of the National Gallery and holding this appointment until 1928. He was knighted in 1921.

Throughout this astonishing sequence he went on painting. His landscapes were mainly of the bleak mountains and industrial scenes of the north of England, where he had been born.

Another who contributed to the work of the war artists in France was HERBERT HUGHES-STANTON (1870–1937). He was a straightforward landscape painter in oils and watercolour, and the work he did in France was exactly what might have been expected – straightforward landscapes of the devastated towns and village of northern France. Another Chelsea-born artist, he was the son of a painter, William Hughes, with whom he trained in his formative years. An ARA in 1913, he proceeded to RA in 1920 and was knighted in 1923.

Tanks were a complete novelty in World War I. They were developed originally by the Royal Navy, encouraged by the imaginative First Lord of the Admiralty, Churchill. Their original purpose was to break the deadlock of trench warfare, for they were able to flatten barbed-wire entanglements, ignore machine-gun fire and straddle trenches; for this reason they were once known as land-ships. Subsequently the name tanks was given as a cover for security purposes. These machines were available only to the British during the war, and they had begun to prove their effectiveness before the end of the conflict. But having invented them, the nation largely neglected them in the post-war years – with tragic results.

The Imperial War Museum rightly considered that they represented an aspect of warfare which should be recorded pictorially. Tanks form the sole subject of BERNARD ADENEY's (1878–1966) pictures in the museum. He was a painter in oils and watercolour, and also a textile designer. He had trained at the Royal Academy Schools, at the Slade and at the Académie Julian. A member of the London Group from 1913, he was its president from 1918 to 1923. He taught at the Central School for more than forty years from 1903, with a wartime interruption in which he served as a gunner in the Tank Corps.

Salonika, in Macedonia, was a minor theatre of war. During the years in which British troops were engaged there, the authorities were not able to do a great deal to ensure that this front would not be neglected in the post-war assembly of pictures. They were fortunate in finding

W. Bernard Adeney, *Tanks Passing Along a Road in France*
Pen and wash, 10¼ × 14½ ins
Mark IV tanks, first produced in 1917, and Mark Vs, dating from 1918, are detailed with almost diagrammatic precision.

that, as it turned out, artists had been on the spot. Stanley Spencer was one, of course; DARSIE JAPP (1883–1973) was another. Japp served in the Royal Artillery, commanding a battery in Macedonia and winning the Military Cross. He was born in Liverpool and had been to St John's College, Oxford. While working in a shipping office he went to evening classes at the Lambeth School of Art, where he was taught by Philip Connard, before moving on to the Slade School as a full-time student from 1908. As it happened he was a Slade contemporary of Stanley Spencer. Darsie Japp did not pursue a career as an artist. He farmed in Berkshire from 1920, later living in France and Spain.

Salonika was also the field of activity of WILLIAM T. WOOD (1877–1958), who became a war artist on that front in 1918. A painter of landscape and flowers in watercolour, Wood had trained at the Regent Street Polytechnic and in Italy. He served in the Royal Flying Corps, partly in the hazardous role of observer in kite balloons.

Represented in the museum by a couple of pictures is the greatly admired WILLIAM NICHOLSON (1872–1949). Today, he is perhaps acclaimed most of all for his still-life paintings: these are deceptively simple pictures, subtly coloured and with an extraordinary intensity, the result of the artist's fine discrimination and sense of tone. He was a versatile artist, an admirable landscape painter, a highly effective

Darsie Japp, *The Royal Field Artillery in Macedonia*
Oil, 72 × 125 ins
The standard field gun of the British army was the 18-pounder, which weighed
2,904 lbs and was normally drawn by a team of six horses, in the same fashion as
the 13-pounders used to this day on ceremonial occasions by the King's Troop,
Royal Artillery.

Sir William Nicholson, *Vice-Admiral Sir William Pakenham, KCB, KCMG, KCVO*
Oil, 50 × 40 ins
A younger son of a younger son of the second Earl of Longford, Pakenham took
command of the Grand Fleet's battle-cruisers when Beatty succeeded Jellicoe as
Commander-in-Chief in November 1916. An austere and dedicated officer,
Pakenham always slept fully dressed at sea, and discarded all cabin furniture except
one chair, to reduce the fire risk.

W. T. Wood, *The Battle of 'The Pips', 24 April 1917*
Watercolour, 22¾ × 33 ins
'The Pips' or 'Pips Ridge' was a strongly fortified German and Bulgarian position
near Lake Doiran. It was assaulted at night by the 22nd and 26th divisions, but the
battle was a costly failure.

Ernest Proctor, *Nieuport Bains, 1918*
Lithograph, 17 × 21½ ins
Nieuport Bains is on the Belgian coast, about ten miles south-west of Ostend, on the estuary of the Yser. Protected by the deliberate flooding of the land to the east of the Yser, Nieuport was in Allied hands throughout the war.

portraitist, a master of woodcuts, of poster and theatre design – he designed the original sets and costumes for *Peter Pan* in 1904, for example.

Trained at von Herkomer's school at Bushey and at the Académie Julian, he made a name for himself in the 1890s, in partnership with his brother-in-law James Pryde, as the poster-designing 'Beggarstaff Brothers'. His fame grew at the turn of the century with his sets of woodcuts, most of all for the woodcut portrait of Queen Victoria, once aptly described as an 'animated tea-cosy'. Knighted in 1936, William Nicholson was the father of the abstract painter Ben Nicholson.

J. D. REVEL (1884–1967) served in Mesopotamia during the war, and later contributed more than thirty watercolours to the museum's collection to help illustrate the fighting on this remote front. A painter in oils and watercolour of portraits and figures, he was born in Dundee

J. D. Revel, *Risaldar, Guides Cavalry (Pathan)*
Watercolour, 19½ × 20 ins
The rank of risaldar in Indian cavalry regiments equated to that of subedar in the infantry. The Guides served in the Mesopotamian campaign. Early history of this famous regiment emerges from the novel *The Far Pavilions* by M. M. Kaye.

and studied at the Royal College of Art. From 1912 head of the Chelsea School of Art, and then moved director of the Glasgow School of Art.

Army life behind the front line, stretching as far back was the province of ERNEST PROCTOR (1886–1935) – thi bution to the museum's collection. A painter of figures ai he had trained at Newlyn and in Paris, later teaching t Glasgow School of Art. An ARA in 1932, he died young, perhaps before his full potential as an artist had been fulfilled.

A youthful prodigy as a painter and an illustrator, AUSTIN OSMAN SPARE (1886–1958) started exhibiting, at the Royal Academy, at the age of sixteen. He trained at Lambeth School of Art and at the Royal College of Art. His work in the museum's collection is concentrated entirely on the labours of the Royal Army Medical Corps, a very important aspect of the wartime army, in view of the very large numbers of casualties throughout the war.

There are two dozen or so sketches in the museum by R. BORLASE SMART (1881–1947); he was a painter, etcher and poster-designer, a member of the St Ives School for many years. He also wrote about seascape painting, at which he was expert, although his work was not confined to the sea. Nevertheless he was perhaps rather unfortunate not to be absorbed into the Royal Navy's embrace as a war artist. The sketches were all made when the artist was serving in France, where he reached the rank of captain in the Machine-Gun Corps.

IAN STRANG (1886–1952), a former Slade School and Académie Julian

Austin O. Spare, *The First Field Dressing*
Pastel, 20 × 30 ins
All troops carried first field dressings. This soldier is attending to a superficial leg wound, surrounded by a dead German soldier and the familiar jumble of an army at war: a discarded gas-mask, a stick grenade, and his own 'small pack' and water-bottle.

R. Borlase Smart, *A Derelict Tank Caught on the Edge of a Shell-hole: near Bouleaux Wood*
Charcoal and watercolour, 12 × 18 ins
Bouleaux Wood was almost in the centre of the Somme battlefield, about seven miles north-west of Peronne. It was captured during the course of September and October 1916. The tank is a Mark I, with its characteristic trailing steering wheels; it was the only model available in 1916.

Ian Strang, *The Menin Road*
Pen and watercolour, 10 × 14 ins
Like Paul Nash, this artist was profoundly moved by the battered landscape (see page 48); but Nash's portrayal of the scene is more powerful, perhaps because he had served in this district as a soldier.

Leon Underwood, *Erecting a Camouflage Tree*
Oil, 42 × 60 ins
The purpose of an imitation tree, made of steel, was as an observation post. There is a German-made specimen in the Imperial War Museum.

student, enlisted in 1914 in the Middlesex Regiment. Commissioned in the Royal Berkshire Regiment in 1915, he served for the rest of the war on the Western Front. During these years he sketched whenever opportunity served: nearly four dozen of these sketches are in the museum's collection.

LEON UNDERWOOD (1890–1975) was both a painter and a sculptor and has paintings in the museum's collection. He had trained at the Royal College of Art and enlisted in 1914, serving in France from 1916 and ending the war as a captain in the Royal Artillery. In the post-war years he switched his activities almost entirely to sculpture.

A sculptor, draughtsman and painter, DERWENT WOOD (1871–1926) has some works of sculpture in the museum's collection. Born in Keswick, he trained in Germany before proceeding to the Royal College of Art and the Royal Academy Schools. From 1897 to 1901 he taught at the Glasgow School of Art. An ARA in 1910, he served

throughout the war in the Royal Army Medical Corps, where he became involved in plastic surgery. Professor of sculpture at the Royal College from 1918 to 1923, and an RA in 1920, he was prolific with portrait busts, statues and, of course, war memorials.

The position of women in the country was radically altered by force of circumstances during the war. With millions of men in the Forces, and with the huge casualty lists, a shortage of 'manpower' developed. The authorities were obliged to call on the help of women. The Forces arranged for women to be enlisted into special units arranged for the purpose. A Women's Land Army was created. Even more than this, women started doing work in what had previously been male preserves. Very large numbers of workers in munitions factories were women. Women also appeared as bus-conductors, window-cleaners, or indeed in almost any job at all. It was during the war, also, that many thousands of firms started employing female secretaries and typists for the first time.

The Imperial War Museum authorities recognised the significance of this and made efforts for women's work to be recorded pictorially. One of those used for this work was, appropriately enough, ANNA AIRY (1882–1964), who had been at the Slade School for four years from 1899. She was an accomplished painter in oils, watercolour and pastels of portraits, figures, genre and still-life.

Women at work is also the theme of the well-known Newlyn School painter STANHOPE FORBES' only picture in the museum's collection, *WRNS Ratings Sail-making*. Forbes (1857–1947) had trained at the RA Schools and had exhibited there from 1885, becoming an RA in 1910.

Another artist largely concerned with women's work was A. S. HARTRICK (1864–1950), an interesting if not very well-known painter. He had an extensive education at Edinburgh University, the Slade School and in France, where he encountered both van Gogh and Gauguin. Returning to Scotland, he became involved with the Glasgow School. As well as being a painter, he also became an illustrator, for *The Graphic* amongst others, from 1889. A member of the New English Art Club, he lived latterly in Gloucestershire, painting mainly landscapes, and teaching at both the Camberwell and Central schools.

Only incidentally concerned with women's work was RANDOLPH SCHWABE (1885–1948), whose twenty-one pictures in the museum's collection are concerned with aspects of work on the land. This became of vital national importance, especially when the U-boat

Francis Derwent Wood, *Marshal Foch*
Plaster, 15½ ins
Almost throughout the war, the Allies in France suffered from lack of unified control. It was not until disaster threatened during the great German attack of March 1918, that unified command was accepted. Although not so called at the time, the Supreme Commander was the French Marshal Ferdinand Foch (1851–1929).

Anna Airy, *Shop for Machining 15-inch shells*
Oil, 72 × 84 ins
A scene in the works of the Singer Manufacturing Company, Clydebank. The enormous shells are being made in a workshop entirely staffed by women, under the supervision of a solitary foreman. The guns which fired these shells were all on battleships; two are still to be seen outside the Imperial War Museum. The shells weighed 1,920 lbs.

Stanhope Forbes, *WRNS Ratings Sail-making*
Oil, 42 × 54 ins
On board HMS *Essex* at Devonport, 1918. HMS *Essex* was an armoured cruiser
dating from 1901. Sails were needed for the ship's boats. The WRNS would not, of
course, have gone to sea, but were no doubt on board for this specific purpose.

campaign was at its most effective and food supplies ran dangerously low. Some of the work done on the land was by the Women's Land Army, some by German prisoners-of-war. Schwabe, an etcher and lithographer in the traditional manner, had trained at the Slade School, the Royal College of Art, and at the Académie Julian in Paris. After the war, he taught at the Royal College before succeeding Tonks as head of the Slade School.

Munitions factories were the province of JOSEPH PENNELL (1858–1926). Pennell was an American, who was born and educated in Philadelphia and who died in Brooklyn. For much of his life, however, he was based in London, where he had a high reputation as an etcher and lithographer, mainly of architectural and topographical subjects. He illustrated many books, notably about travel, and he wrote travel books as well, sometimes with his wife as co-author. The two of them collaborated in writing the official life of their fellow-American expatriate, the artist James McNeill Whistler, who died in 1903.

Randolph Schwabe, *Voluntary Land Workers in a Flax-field*
Oil, 42 × 60 ins
The flax industry in Britain had been revived to meet the special needs of the Royal Flying Corps. The camouflaged bell tents to house the harvesters were evidently provided by the military authorities.

Joseph Pennell, *Bringing in the Gun*
Lithograph, 19¾ × 15¼ ins
One of the artist's many dramatic and skilful lithographs of aspects of the 'Home Front'.

Archibald Hartrick, *A Lift Girl*
Lithograph in two colours, 16¼ × 10 ins
One of a series for the Underground Railway Company. The subsidiary drawing shows the soldiers' habit of naming trenches, often after well-known London streets.

BUILDING A NEW WORLD?

World War I changed many things, but it is often hard to discern exactly what. With comfortable hindsight it is clear that, in many cases, it did not so much instigate change as accelerate a process which would have happened anyway – although not at such a pace – even if no war had occurred. The development of aircraft is a well-known example of this: the military authorities in all the countries involved in the war rapidly abandoned their notion that aeroplanes were simply expensive playthings, and their demands forced through research and developments which might otherwise have taken decades to emerge in an atmosphere controlled by normal commercial considerations.

Occasionally it can be seen plainly that specific changes were direct results of the war. The position of women in British society is an obvious example. It was the contribution made by women towards the national war effort which changed official attitudes. Even before the war had ended, unopposed legislation had given votes to women in national elections (at first only to those aged over thirty), adding thereby more than eight million voters. This change in the franchise certainly altered the political landscape permanently and decisively.

A more subtle, though no less permanent, example of change in the political set-up caused by the war came from its nature as a national conflict, a total war eventually embracing all aspects of life. It became natural to suppose that, in such circumstances, government direction of affairs was normal and necessary, where previously any kind of official direction would have been considered outrageously and unthinkably interfering. The wartime Ministries of Health, of Labour and of Transport, for example, survived the end of the war and continued their wartime functions in peacetime. They exist today, albeit submerged in larger ministries.

Changes in the way people lived were undoubtedly affected by the war. Women's fashions in the post-war years, with short hairstyles and flattened chests, derived in part from the fact that, in the war years, millions of women had done jobs previously performed exclusively by men. Perhaps it was also something of a protest against the fact that they had often been obliged to give up these jobs when the huge process of demobilisation released millions of men from their wartime service in the forces.

Women now began smoking cigarettes, perhaps in imitation of men. Men's smoking habits changed, too. In Edwardian days, the gentry had smoked Havana cigars, while working men smoked pipes; after the war, cigarettes became far more universal. This was largely because the habit had spread in the army, where the supply of cigarettes was always regarded as a priority. Similarly, contraceptive sheaths, made available to troops in France and elsewhere as a means of reducing the high incidence of venereal diseases, first introduced the working man to methods of contraception previously known only to the middle classes.

The playing of the National Anthem at the end of every concert,

every theatrical performance, even every performance in a cinema which had been introduced as a patriotic gesture during the war, persisted into peace, lasting indeed throughout the inter-war years and through World War II, and not withering away until the 1960s.

The gigantic numbers of casualties, however, were in themselves the most pervasive post-war influence – not least in that they exaggerated greatly the existing surplus of women in the community. In the field of politics, they not only inspired the pacifist movement but also dominated much of the thinking of those in authority between the wars. A horror of the prospect of casualties on the scale of the war was very prevalent in international affairs. Twenty years after the Armistice, it was, for example, implicit in the Munich Agreement of 1938; and we should remember in this connection that French casualty figures from the war were almost double those of Britain, even though the population of France was smaller.

Reminders of wartime losses were a constant and potent element in ordinary lives in the 1920s and the 1930s. The two-minute silence, always observed in those years at 11am on 11 November itself (rather than on the nearest Sunday, as is now the case) was immensely impressive. It was signalled by maroons fired from police stations, and everything stopped across the whole country until a second bang indicated the end of the two minutes. This happened not just at services by war memorials and in churches, but everywhere – all traffic, all movement in the streets came to a standstill, all trains, shops and offices, all work in factories, all teaching in schools; everything stopped. Stillness was complete. Silence was universal.

War memorials, always in prominent places, were in themselves another element. In Britain, as in France, with their sometimes hideous appearance, their neat gardens, their carefully compiled lists of names, ranks and regiments, they are to this day a feature of every town and village, as well as of institutions, schools, colleges and offices. They can still touch the heart-strings with their poignant, pathetic messages.

If so much else was changed by World War I, was art affected? Certainly many of the artists were changed. While men like Muirhead Bone, Lavery and Clausen were well able to pick up their careers without undue stress or difficulty, this was by no means always the case. For some, the direct effects of the war made it impossible. Orpen is an example here, since his career declined rapidly after his traumatic experience at the Peace Conference; the war had affected him decisively and tragically. This was the case, naturally enough, with many others. Nevinson is another example: seeming to find his greatest fulfilment in his wartime work, in later years he was widely thought never to have achieved all that he had promised. His success as a war artist was a personal tragedy. Many others, like Stanley Spencer, took time to readjust.

Others felt the influence of the war in the opposite direction, as it were. For some of the younger men, such as Philpot and the Nash brothers, it was their wartime pictures which first brought them wide public attention. The war can rightly be said to have made their careers.

Some artists, then, were changed; some were changed radically; and some were scarcely affected. But what of art itself? In the whole history of British art, the official art of World War I does not, of itself, play a significant part. As this account has shown, it is a largely haphazard accumulation of many diverse strains, with contributions from artists of diverse persuasions and temperaments. It is not even a fully representative assembly of British art of the time. We shall never know what responses to war might have come from Sickert (Steer's contemporary), from stalwarts of the Camden Town Group such as Gilman, Ginner and Bevan, or what might have been made of it by Wadsworth, Matthew Smith or (fascinating thought) L. S. Lowry, who was twenty-seven in 1914. We can only conjecture.

Those movements in art which had been so important a feature of artistic life in continental Europe in the early years of the century, had just begun to find a response in Britain by the time that war erupted in 1914. But those responses would have developed, with or without a war. Possibly the war helped a little, in that, as has been shown, unfamiliarly modern work was first introduced to a wider public through the medium of exhibitions of war artists' work. But, equally, the exigencies of war artists' work may have slowed things down: working under censorship and to the order of authority is not a natural or satisfactory state of affairs for an artist. And to this general constriction must be added such instructions as were given to Roberts about the inadmissibility of Cubist work (page 69). Although artists individually were affected by the war, the consequences for art itself were minimal.

BIBLIOGRAPHY

Benezit, E.	Dictionnaire des Peintres, Sculpteurs, Dessinateurs et Graveurs	1976
Blunden, Edmund	Undertones of War	1928
Bone, Muirhead	The Western Front	1917
Chamot, Mary; Farr, Dennis; and Butlin, Martin	Tate Gallery Catalogues: The Modern British Paintings, Drawings and Sculpture	1964
Churchill, Winston S.	The World Crisis	revised 1931
Clark, Kenneth	Another Part of the Wood	1974
Dangerfield, George	The Strange Death of Liberal England	1935
Easton, Malcolm and Holroyd, Michael	The Art of Augustus John	1974
Eksteins, Modris	Rites of Spring	1989
Farr, Dennis	English Art, 1870–1940	1978
Ferguson, John	The Arts in Britain in World War I	1980
Forester, C. S.	The General	1937
Graves, Robert	Goodbye to All That	1929
Harries, Meiron and Susie	The War Artists	1983
Hemingway, Ernest	A Farewell to Arms	1929
Holme, Charles	The War: Depicted by Distinguished British Artists	1918
Holroyd, Michael	Augustus John	1974–5
	Lytton Strachey	1967–8

Horne, Alistair	The Price of Glory	1962
Montague, C. E.	Disenchantment	1922
Nowell-Smith, Simon (ed)	Edwardian England, 1901–1914	1964
Orpen, William	An Onlooker in France	revised 1924
Pennell, Joseph	Pictures of War Work in England	1917
Powell, Anthony	To Keep the Ball Rolling	1976–8, 1980–2
Remarque, E. M.	All Quiet on the Western Front	1929
Rothenstein, John	British Artists and the War	1931
	Modern English Painters	revised 1976
St John, John	William Heinemann	1990
Sassoon, Siegfried	Memoirs of an Infantry Officer	1930
Sherriff, R. C.	Journey's End	1928
Sillars, Stuart	Art and Survival in First World War Britain	1987
Taylor, A. J. P.	England 1914–1945	1965
Thomson, David	England in the Twentieth Century	1965
Tuchman, Barbara	The Guns of August	1962
Tucker, John F.	Johnny Get Your Gun	1978
Van der Dat, Dan	The Ship that Changed the World	1986
Waters, Grant	Dictionary of British Artists working 1900–1950	1975
Wilkinson, Norman	The Dardenelles: Colour Sketches from Gallipoli	1915
Woodward, E. L.	History of England	1947

INDEX